Works 2000
Made Simple

P.K.McBride

MADE SIMPLE
BOOKS

OXFORD AUCKLAND BOSTON JOHANNESBURG MELBOURNE NEW DELHI

Made Simple
An imprint of Butterworth-Heinemann
Linacre House, Jordan Hill, Oxford OX2 8DP
225 Wildwood Avenue, Woburn MA 01801-2041
A division of Reed Educational and Professional Publishing Ltd

Q A member of the Reed Elsevier plc group

First published 2000
© P K McBride 2000

TRADEMARKS/REGISTERED TRADEMARKS
Computer hardware and software brand names mentioned in this book
are protected by their respective trademarks and are acknowledged.

British Library Cataloguing in Publication Data
A catalogue record for this book is available from the British Library.

ISBN 0 7506 4985 2

Typeset by Elle and P.K.McBride, Southampton, UK
Icons designed by Sarah Ward © 1994

Transferred to digital printing 2005

Printed and bound by Antony Rowe Ltd, Eastbourne

Contents

Preface

Works is an integrated suite, developed for the SoHo market. Let's try that again in English... Works is a set of programs, designed for the Small Office/Home Office users. The integration works at three levels.

- All use the same common set of core commands, so that when you have mastered one program, you are half way to mastery of the next.

- Any number of documents, from the same or different tools, can be in use at the same, so that you can flick quickly from one job to another.

- Data can be transferred freely between them, so that charts created from a spreadsheet can be copied into a report; lists of names and addresses, organised in the database can be merged with a standard letter to produce a customised mailing; word-processed memos can be taken into communications and zipped off down the phone line.

This book covers Works 2000, the latest version of this excellent suite. It has Task Wizards to simplify the creation of all manner of documents, and extensive on-screen Help. These, on top of an already user-friendly system, makes Works an ideal package for people who want to get things done – but don't want to have to spend too long learning how.

The book assumes that you have Works 2000 already installed on your PC, and that you have mastered the basic skills for using Windows – if you do need help with the basics, you might like to try *Windows 98 Made Simple* or *Windows ME Made Simple*.

1 Starting work

Great works...

Word processor

Use this to write your letters, reports, newsletters and novels. The range of facilities on offer almost makes this a desktop publishing (DTP) package. There are a wide range of typefaces, font styles and sizes, to be used for headings and for emphasis; headers, footers and page numbers can be added; text can be laid out in columns; and graphics, charts and tables can be placed in the text.

Spreadsheet

Use this to manage your cheque book, payroll, cash flow and all other aspects of your accounts – or anything else that involves numbers and calculations. With its DTP facilities, you can also use it for invoices and estimates.

Database

Use this to manage your stock, organize your address book or other sets of data. If any calculations are needed, this will produce a range of summary values, and data can be easily transferred between here and the spreadsheet.

... and lesser works

Works also includes **Calendar**, which can help you to keep track of appointments, meetings, birthdays and other events.

The Task Launcher gives you quick access to your **Address Book**, **Internet Explorer** and **Outlook Express**.

Other tools

- ❑ These can be used within the main Works programs.

Clip Art manages a gallery of graphics that can be inserted into documents. Some are supplied with Works, and you can add your own.

Drawing lets you create diagrams and annotated illustrations.

Graph lets you produce pie charts, line, bar and other graphs.

Painting brings Windows Paint into a Works document.

WordArt lets you create special effects, such as slanting or curved text, perhaps with shadows or other trimmings, for labels and headings.

The Task Launcher

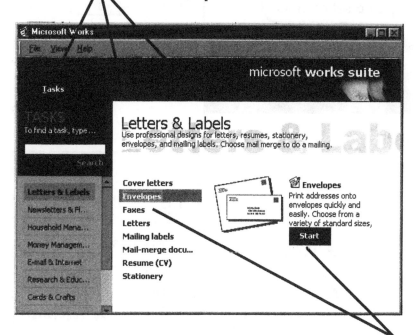

Take note

On the Tasks and Programs tabs, you can often find a suitable Task with a keyword search — just type a word or two to describe what you want to do and click **Search**.

When you first come into Works, and whenever you set out to create a new document, you will meet the **Task Launcher** dialog box. This has three panels:

- **Tasks.** These create ready-formatted blank documents into which you can write your own text or data. The documents include letters – for many different purposes – invoices, address books, inventories, CVs, budgeting and more. If calculations are needed, the formulae are already there; all have text styles, colours and layouts ready set. And if the documents are not exactly what you want, they can be tailored to suit (see page 4).

- **Programs.** Use this tab to start a new word processor, spreadsheet or database document from scratch.

- **History.** Use this to open a Works document that you created in an earlier session (see page 13).

Click on the label to open its panel

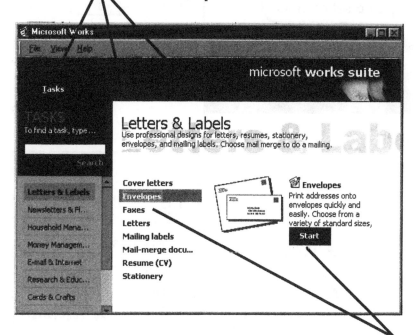

Click to select then click Start

Starting from Tasks

Any time that you want to produce a new document – of any type – check out the Tasks first. These cover many of the jobs that home users often want to perform on their computers.

When you start a task, you may just be asked to select from a small set of options, and Works will then open the relevant *template* – a document with the formatting and basic information in place, waiting for you to customise it and add your own information. Other Tasks run Wizards to ask for option choices and other information before setting up the document for you.

The same tasks are available on the **Tasks** tab, where they are organised by the type of job, and the **Programs** tab, where they are grouped according to the program that is used.

Basic steps

1 In the Task Launcher switch to the Tasks (or Programs) tab.

2 Click on a category heading (or program name) to display its set of tasks.

3 Select a task, then click Start.

4 Set the options and enter information as required.

5 Click [Next >] after each stage.

6 Click [< Back] if you want to redo a stage.

7 Click [Finish] at the end.

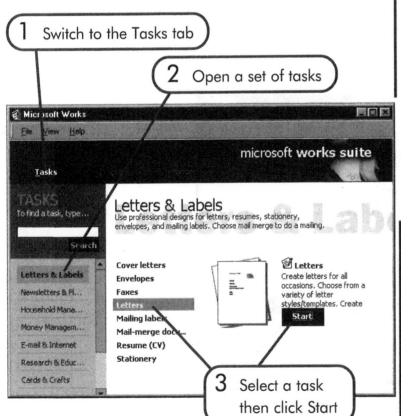

1 Switch to the Tasks tab

2 Open a set of tasks

3 Select a task then click Start

Tip

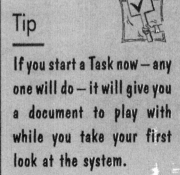

If you start a Task now — any one will do — it will give you a document to play with while you take your first look at the system.

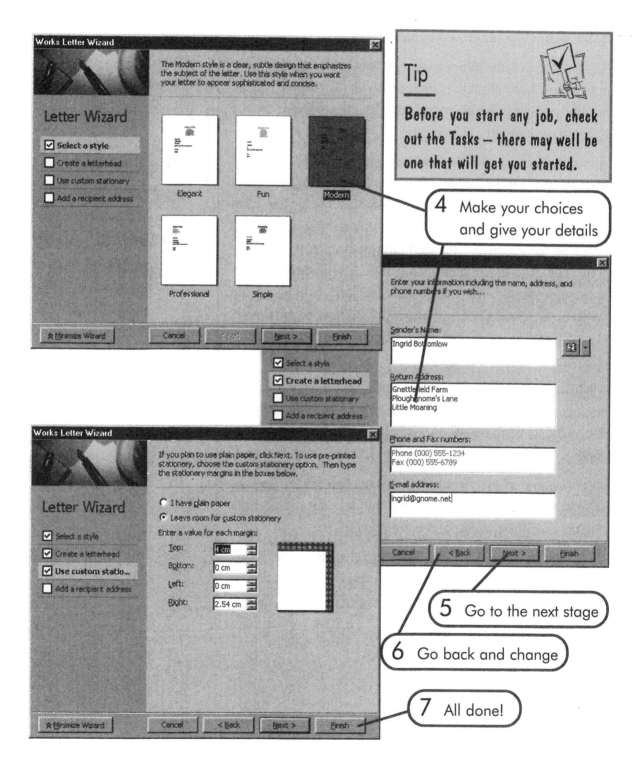

Works Letter Wizard

The Modern style is a clear, subtle design that emphasizes the subject of the letter. Use this style when you want your letter to appear sophisticated and concise.

Letter Wizard

☑ Select a style
☐ Create a letterhead
☐ Use custom stationery
☐ Add a recipient address

Elegant   Fun   Modern

Professional   Simple

⊼ Minimize Wizard   Cancel   < Back   Next >   Finish

Tip

Before you start any job, check out the Tasks — there may well be one that will get you started.

④ Make your choices and give your details

☑ Select a style
☑ Create a letterhead
☐ Use custom stationery
☐ Add a recipient address

Enter your information including the name, address, and phone numbers if you wish...

Sender's Name:
Ingrid Bottomlow

Return Address:
Gnettlefield Farm
Ploughgnome's Lane
Little Moaning

Phone and Fax numbers:
Phone (000) 555-1234
Fax (000) 555-6789

E-mail address:
ingrid@gnome.net

Cancel   < Back   Next >   Finish

Works Letter Wizard

If you plan to use plain paper, click Next. To use pre-printed stationery, choose the custom stationery option. Then type the stationery margins in the boxes below.

Letter Wizard

☑ Select a style
☑ Create a letterhead
☑ Use custom statio...
☐ Add a recipient address

○ I have plain paper
● Leave room for custom stationery

Enter a value for each margin:

Top: 4 cm
Bottom: 0 cm
Left: 0 cm
Right: 2.54 cm

⊼ Minimize Wizard   Cancel   < Back   Next >   Finish

⑤ Go to the next stage

⑥ Go back and change

⑦ All done!

5

The desktop

Think of the Works screen as your desktop.

The main area – the **Workspace** – is where you lay out your documents. Each of these is in its own window, which can be minimised out of the way, or tucked beneath or to the side of the one you are currently working on.

Above the workspace is the **Toolbar**, containing buttons which can call up the most frequently used commands. Most aspects of font styles and settings, and alignment can be set from here. If a button is highlighted, it means that its setting is currently active. In the screenshot, the **Left alignment** button is the only active one. As a single click on one of these will replace two or three selections through menus, they are well worth using. In the spreadsheet and database you can add buttons to the Toolbar, or remove those you do not use. (See *Customizing the toolbar*, page 76.)

At the top of the screen is the **Menu Bar**, and the menus that can be pulled down from here, carry the full range of commands. The contents of the menu bar vary slightly from one tool to another. (See *The menu system*, page 8.)

At the bottom of the screen is the **Status Bar**. When you are selecting from menus or the toolbar buttons, this carries brief reminders of the purpose of the commands.

To the right of the screen is the **Help panel**. This can be shrunk out of the way to make more working space if you need it, or opened to give easy access to help. (See Chapter 2, *Getting Help*.)

Tip

Hold the pointer for a moment over a toolbar button or a menu option, and a *Tool Tip* will appear to tell you what it does.

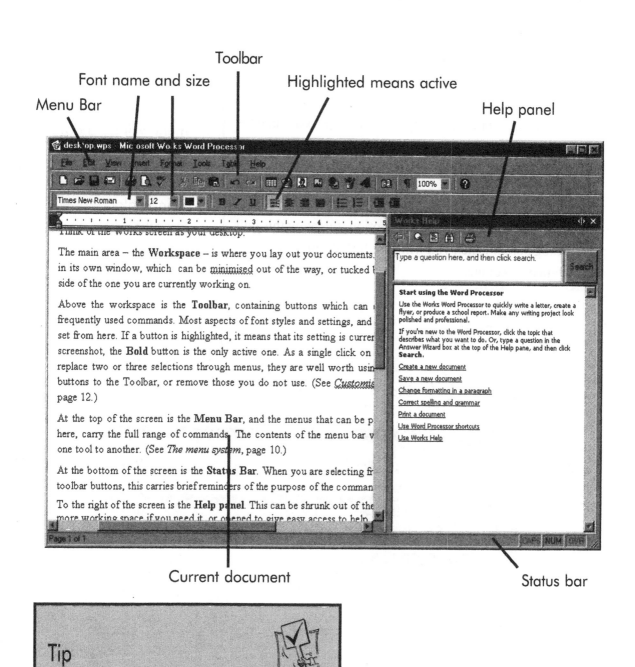

Menu Bar

Font name and size

Toolbar

Highlighted means active

Help panel

Current document

Status bar

The menu system

All of Works' facilities can be accessed through the menu system. The commands are grouped under more-or-less appropriate headings. The fit isn't quite perfect because not every command falls into a neat category. But finding a command is rarely a problem.

If you see a **tick** to the left of a menu option, it means that this is a toggle (on/off) switch, and that it is currently turned on.

If you see an ellipsis (**...**) after a menu option, selecting this will open a dialog box in which you will give further information or make detailed selections.

Basic steps

❑ To select commands

1 Point to a heading in the Menu bar and its menu will drop down.

2 If you do not see what you want, move the pointer along, opening other menus.

3 When you find the command you want, click to select it.

❑ To abort selection

4 Click anywhere else on screen to close the menu.

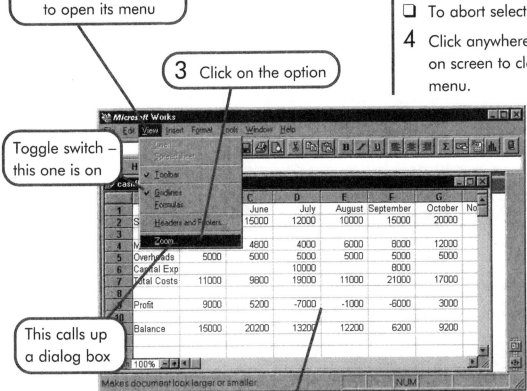

1 Click on a heading to open its menu

3 Click on the option

Toggle switch – this one is on

This calls up a dialog box

4 Click off the menu to abandon

Basic steps

❑ To select commands

1 Hold down [Alt]. This tells the system to expect a key selection.

2 Press the underlined letter of the header to open the menu.

3 Press the underlined letter of the menu option.

❑ To abort selection

4 Press [Esc].

Selecting with keys

When you are typing in data, it is sometimes simpler to make your menu selections with the keys, rather than with the mouse. Some of the commonly used commands have **[Control]** key combination shortcuts, but all can be accessed via the **[Alt]** key.

The quickest method is to use the key letter of the menu choices, but if you want to browse, or use the **[Left]** and **[Right]** arrow keys to move along the menu bar and the **[Up]** and **[Down]** arrows to move the highlight to the option you want. Pressing **[Enter]** selects the highlighted option.

Keyboard shortcut

Tip
___
Watch out for the keyboard shortcuts.

4 Press [Esc] to abort

2 Press the underlined letter to select

Use either [Enter] key

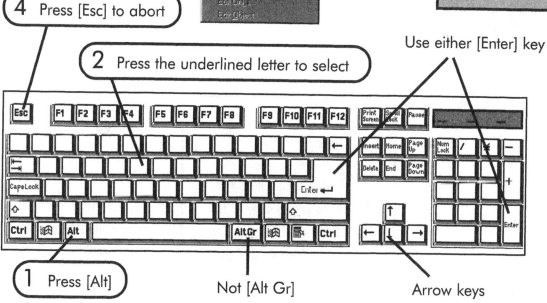

1 Press [Alt]

Not [Alt Gr]

Arrow keys

9

Saving files

While you are working on a document, its data is stored in the computer's memory. When you exit from Works, or switch of the machine, the memory is wiped. Sometimes, that can be a good thing. Do you really want to keep all those Thank You letters that you wrote after last Christmas? As long as you have sent printed copies off to your friends and relatives, you have no further use of them.

More often, perhaps, you will want to keep a copy of the document for reference, or to do some more work on in future. To do this, you must save it to disk.

The process is the same, whatever the type of document, and very simple. All you really have to do is decide on which disk and in which folder it will be stored, and what you will call it.

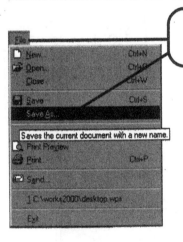

1 Open the File menu and select Save or Save As...

Take note

If you have edited a document and want to keep a copy of the original, as well as the new version, use Save As and give it a different name.

☐ To save a new file

1 Open the File menu and select Save or Save As... or click on the toolbar.

2 The first time you save a file, the Save As... dialog box will appear to collect the details.

3 Select the Drive and the Folder.

4 Leave the File Type alone, unless you want to export the document for use with a different software package.

5 Type in a File Name.

6 Click ▭ Save ▭.

☐ To resave a file

Use File – Save or click ▭.

☐ To save a file under a new name

Open the File menu and select Save As... then continue as for a new file.

Extensions

❑ The Works extensions:

wps Word Processor

wdb Database

wks Spreadsheet

wcm Communications

❑ Other extensions that
you may meet:

wmf Windows
MetaFile (for Clip Art)

bmp BitMap from
Paintbrush or other art
programs

txt Text file from
Notepad or another
word processor

doc Microsoft Word
document – Works
can read those from
Word (up to version
6.0)

Tip

If you have created headed notepaper, an
invoice or other document that you will want
to reuse – with different text – in future,
save it as a Template (see page 14).

File names

There are two parts to every file name – the **name** itself and a
three-letter **extension**. The name is given by you to a file when
you save it. Windows sets no limits on the length or the
characters you can use in file names, but:

● the name must not be the same as an existing file in the
same folder (or the new will overwrite the old).

● the name must *mean something to you*.

Don't bother about the extension. Leave it to Works to add a
suitable one to identify the nature of the file.

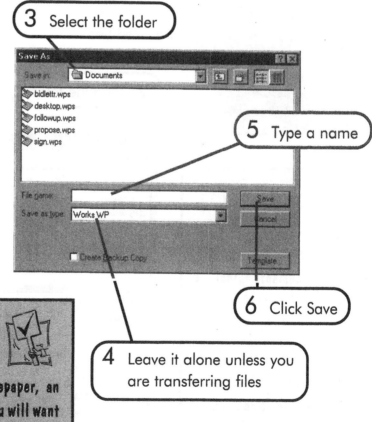

3 Select the folder

5 Type a name

6 Click Save

4 Leave it alone unless you
are transferring files

Opening files

To get your documents back at the start of your next working session, you must open their files. Opening them is easy enough. The tricky part may well be *finding* them, especially as time goes by and your files start to run into their hundreds. However, Works goes a long way to make even this relatively painless.

❏ From within Works

1 Open the File menu and select Open.

2 Set the Drive and Folder, if necessary.

3 Pull down the Type of files list and select the type you want.

4 Click on the file name to select the file.

5 Click ⬛Open⬛.

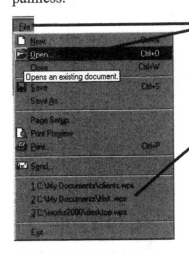

1 Select File – Open

Recently used files are listed here

Tip

Works always starts to Look in the Documents folder. If you have relatively few files, keep them all in there.

If you need to several folders to organise your files, create them within Documents, where you can easily switch into them.

2 Find the folder

4 Select the file

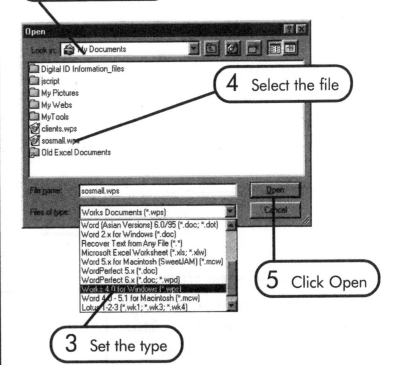

5 Click Open

3 Set the type

Basic steps

❑ From Task Launcher

1 Switch to History tab.

2 Select the file and double-click on it.

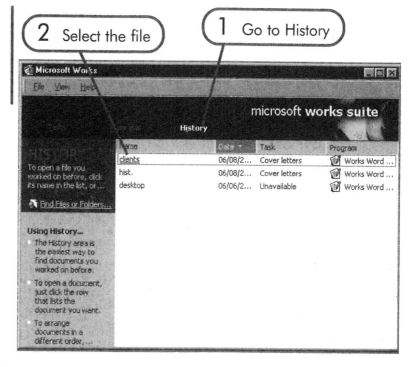

┌─────────────┐   ┌─────────────┐
│ 2 Select the file │   │ 1 Go to History │
└─────────────┘   └─────────────┘

Microsoft Works

File   View   Help

microsoft **works suite**

History

Name	Date ▾	Task	Program
clients	06/08/2...	Cover letters	Works Word ...
hist.	06/08/2...	Cover letters	Works Word ...
desktop	06/06/2...	Unavailable	Works Word ...

HISTORY

To open a file you worked on before, click its name in the list, or ...

Find Files or Folders...

Using History...

• The History area is the easiest way to find documents you worked on before.

• To open a document, just click the row that lists the document you want.

• To arrange documents in a different order, ...

Tip

If you cannot remember where you stored a file, click on the '**Find Files or Folders**' link to go to the File Finder (see page 20).

Transferring files?

If you want to copy a file to or from another machine, running different software, check the alternative file types. There is probably one that will do the job.

● **Word processor** documents can be saved and opened as plain Text or in Word, Wordperfect, WordStar and other formats.

● **Spreadsheets** can be saved or opened as Text or in Excel or Lotus 1-2-3 formats.

● **Databases** can be saved or opened as Text, Comma Separated Text or in dBase formats.

Templates

Tasks offer a quick and easy way to start new documents, but with templates, you have an approach that is even quicker and easier.

A template is a document that has all its formatting and permanent information in place, into which you will type new, specific text and data before printing. Headed notepaper is a simple and obvious example of a template. Others include invoices, quotations, statements, certificates, invitations and thank-you letters. With these and similar formatted 'blanks', the simplest approach is to use a Wizard to produce the first, save it as a template, then load in the template next time you want one.

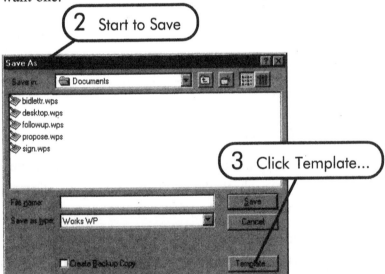

2 Start to Save

3 Click Template...

Basic steps

❑ Saving a template

1 Create the document, with all its formatting and fixed text.

2 Start to save the file with File – Save.

3 At the Save As dialog box, click Template...

4 On the Save As Template dialog box, type a name.

5 Click Default >> to open the lower half of the box to see – or reset – the current defaults.

6 If you want to make the template the default – so that it is used for all new documents (in that tool) – check the box.

Tip

The template does not have to be complicated. It might just set the margins and layout. Use simple ones like this as your defaults if you need a different Page Setup (see page 40) for your word processor, spreadsheet and database documents.

14

7 Click [OK].

❏ Using a template

8 Go to the Tasks panel on the Task Launcher.

9 Select Personal Templates and pick a template from there.

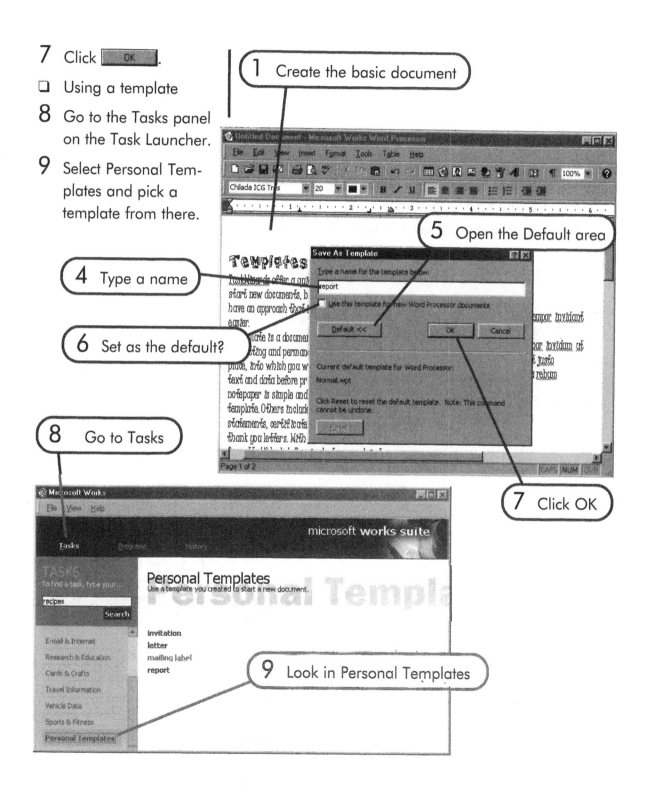

1 Create the basic document

5 Open the Default area

4 Type a name

6 Set as the default?

8 Go to Tasks

7 Click OK

9 Look in Personal Templates

Personal Templates
Use a template you created to start a new document.

invitation
letter
mailing label
report

File Finder

This can track down files by name, type, age, size or contents. As long as you have something to go on, no files need remain lost for long.

Give as much of the name as you can, using an asterisk if you want to leave a gap in the middle; e.g.:

'*DOC*' will find '*doc*ument1', 'Letter to *doc*tor', and any Word files with a .DOC extension;

'REP*.WPS' will find '*Rep*ort156.*wps*', '*Rep*lytoJim.*wps*' and similar files.

1 On the Task Launcher go to the History tab and click the Find Files or Folders... link.

2 Type as much of the Name as you know – if there is identifiable Containing text, you can give this.

3 Tell it where to start to Look in – it will also search the subfolders unless you turn this off.

❏ To narrow searches

4 If you know when you

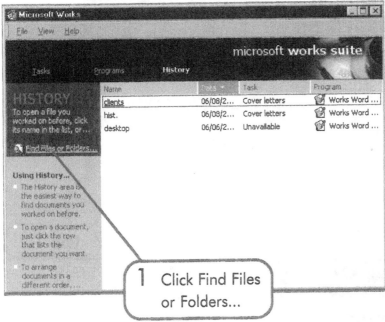

1 Click Find Files or Folders...

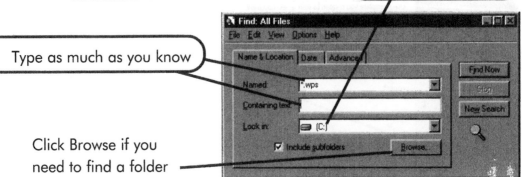

3 Set the start point

2 Type as much as you know

Click Browse if you need to find a folder

last worked on the file,
open the Date panel.

5 Set the between limits
or the previous
months' or days' age.

6 Open the Advanced
panel.

7 Select the type of file
and/or enter its size.

8 Click Find Now to start
the search.

9 Double-click on a
name in the found list
to open the file.

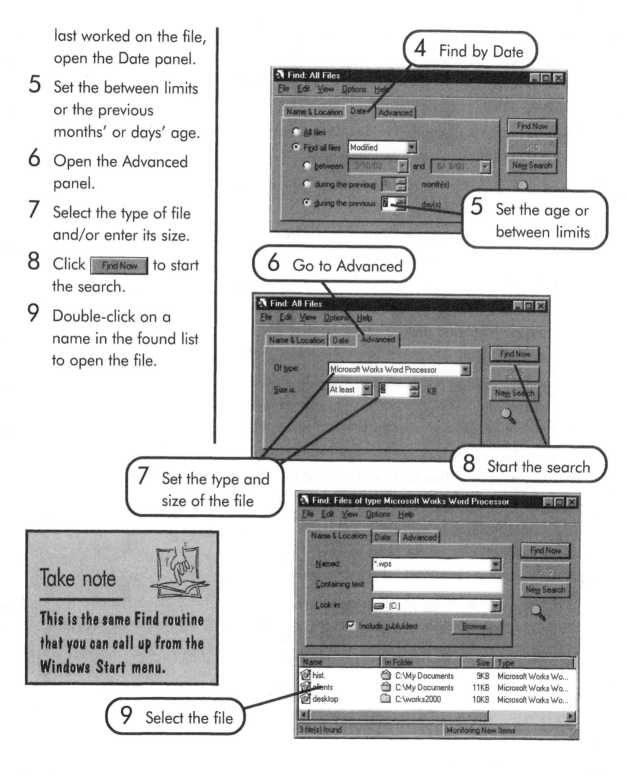

4 Find by Date

5 Set the age or
between limits

6 Go to Advanced

7 Set the type and
size of the file

8 Start the search

9 Select the file

Take note

This is the same Find routine
that you can call up from the
Windows Start menu.

17

Summary

❑ Works contains three main tools, Word Processor, Spreadsheet and Database, plus a Calendar and a set of smaller tools that can be called up from within the main ones.

❑ New documents are started and existing ones opened through the Task Launcher.

❑ Tasks offer a quick and simple way to create a wide variety of documents.

❑ You can open any number of documents from the same or different tools at the same time, though your workspace may get crowded.

❑ All of Works' commands can be reached through the menus. Point and click to select, or type [Alt] followed by the underlined letter in the menu item.

❑ Documents from all the tools are saved by the same File – Save command. If wanted, they can be saved in different formats for transfer to other software.

❑ Existing documents are recalled with File – Open. Works can read in files that were created by other leading applications.

❑ Formatted documents can be saved as Templates, and reopened later as the basis of new documents, with the basic structure and styles already in place.

❑ The Find routine allows you to locate missing files through a combination of partial names, age, type, unique text and size.

2 Getting help

The Help panel

In Works, Help is always at hand. The Help panel is normally open all the time, for instant access. If you need the space more than the Help, it can be shrunk out of the way, or completely hidden. In either case, it can be reopened easily at any point.

Basic steps

1 To hide the Help menu click ■ on the Help panel.

or

2 Click ◀▶ Shrink Help.

❑ Opening Help

3 If the panel has been hidden, click ❷ or use Works Help from the Help menu.

or

4 Click ◀▶ to unshrink.

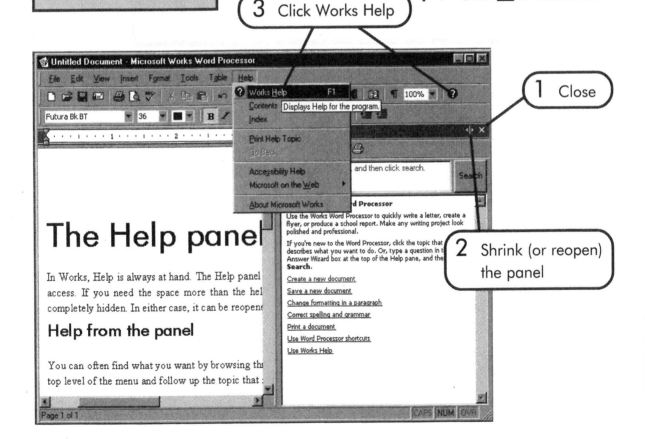

3 Click Works Help

1 Close

2 Shrink (or reopen) the panel

Basic steps

1 Open the Help panel, if necessary.

2 Scroll through the topics.

3 Click on one that meets your needs.

❑ You may then need to select through one or two levels of sub-topics.

4 Work through the Help box.

5 Click on any of the Related topics for extra Help.

Help from the panel

You can often find what you want by browsing through the Help panel. Just start from the top level of the menu and follow up the topic that interests you.

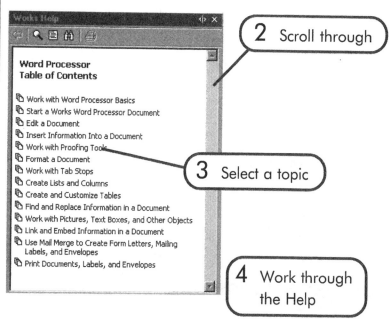

2 Scroll through

3 Select a topic

4 Work through the Help

Click here to step back to the previous list

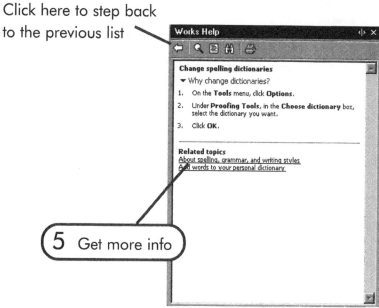

5 Get more info

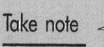

The Help Index

Using the Index can be a quicker way to get to the right information, as long as you know what you are looking for. You don't have to be that exact, as the Help pages are cross-referenced. You can often get to the same page from several different start points, and once into the pages, you can easily switch between related topics.

The **Index** can be reached from the Help menu, or from Help panel.

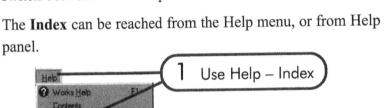

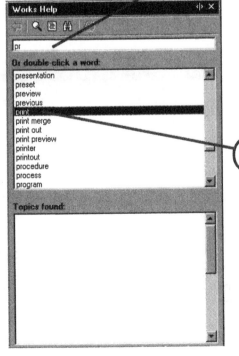

Basic steps

1 Open the Help menu and select Index, or click on the 🔍 Index button on the Help panel.

2 Start to type a word that describes the topic you are interested in. As you type, the list of topics will adjust to show those that start with the same letters.

3 Double-click on a word to get a list of pages related to it.

4 Select a topic from the Topics list.

5 Work through the selected Help page.

Tip

If you can't see anything promising, try a different keyword for the topic

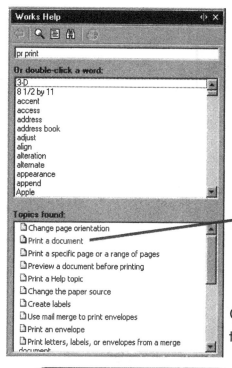

Tip

Press [F1] for instant Help. It will give you a tip when working in a dialog box, and open the Index/Contents panel at other times.

4 Select a topic

You can type in a question and get it to search for an answer – this is the *Answer Wizard*

Click to go back to try another page

5 Work through the Help

If you click on a green word, an explanation of it will be inserted into the text just after it

If you point to a button image, a tool tip will pop up to tell you what it is

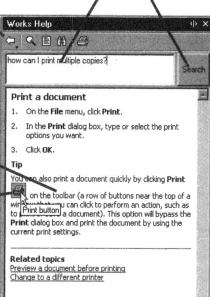

Take note

Some Help pages have links to Related topics listed at the bottom – just click to follow the link.

Help Contents

In the **Contents**, the Help pages are divided into tools, so that you only see the pages for the tool that you are working in at the time. They are then organised into a hierarchy of topics – work your way down through the levels of folders to focus on the help you need.

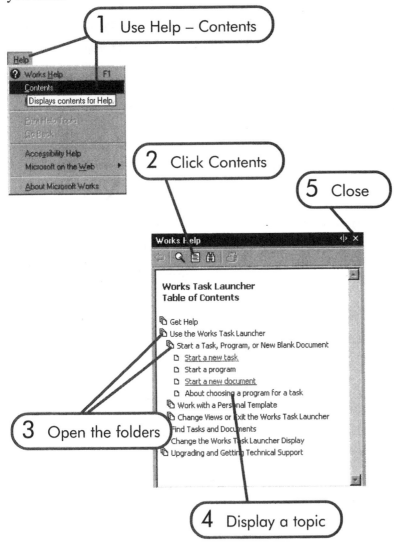

1 Use Help – Contents

2 Click Contents

5 Close

Works Task Launcher
Table of Contents

- Get Help
- Use the Works Task Launcher
  - Start a Task, Program, or New Blank Document
    - □ Start a new task
    - □ Start a program
    - □ Start a new document
    - □ About choosing a program for a task
  - Work with a Personal Template
  - Change Views or Exit the Works Task Launcher
  - Find Tasks and Documents
  - Change the Works Task Launcher Display
  - Upgrading and Getting Technical Support

3 Open the folders

4 Display a topic

1 Open the Help menu and select Contents.

or

2 If the Help panel is open, click 🗐 to switch to the Contents tab.

3 Click on the folders to open (or reclose) them, until you find the topic you want.

4 Click on the topic to display it in the Help panel.

5 Click ⊠ when you have done.

Take note

On some Help pages you will see a brief question or topic header in green with a down arrow beside it. This shows there is more Help available about the sub-topic — click the arrow to display the text.

Basic steps

❑ Help in dialog boxes

1 Click on the ▦ icon at the top right. The icon changes to a query pointer.

2 Point and click on the item that you want to know about. A tip box opens.

3 Click anywhere off the tip box to close it.

Other Help

When working in a dialog box, you can get help on any options within the box.

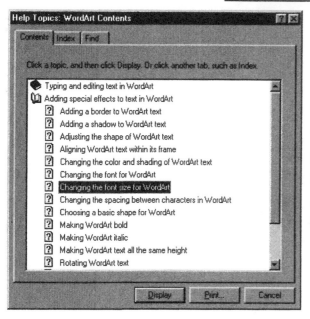

1 Get the query pointer

Adds or removes a border from the bottom edge of the selection.

2 Click on an item

3 Click anywhere to close

Help and the minor works

The Help systems for ClipArt, WordArt and the other minor tools follow the Windows standard – as in the example screenshot here. See *Windows 98 Made Simple* or *Windows ME Made Simple* if you need more help on Help for these.

Summary

❑ Works offers plenty of Help to its users.

❑ The Help panel can be shrunk or hidden if you need more working space.

❑ Help – Index will take you more directly you a Help page, as long as you can describe what you want.

❑ Help – Contents takes you to folders of topics. You will usually have to work through two or three levels of folders to reach a page.

❑ When you are in the Help system, you can go back over previous pages or move around related topics.

❑ Pressing [F1] will open the Index/Contents box or give you a tip on a dialog box.

❑ Dialog boxes carry a Query button to tell you more about the options in the box.

3 Working with text

Starting a new document

When you start a new document, there should be nothing in your main working area, apart from the faint outlines of the text and header (see page 50) areas.

The vertical, flashing, line is the **insertion point**. It marks the place where new text will be inserted when you type or paste it in.

The font name and size, alignment and margins shown on the toolbar and ruler will hold throughout the document – until you change them, though selected words and paragraphs within the document can have their own settings. If you want a significantly different appearance for your document, change the settings at the start.

Tip

The Ruler is very useful for setting margins and tabs – see pages 43 and 45. If it is not displayed on your screen, open the View menu and click to put a tick by Ruler.

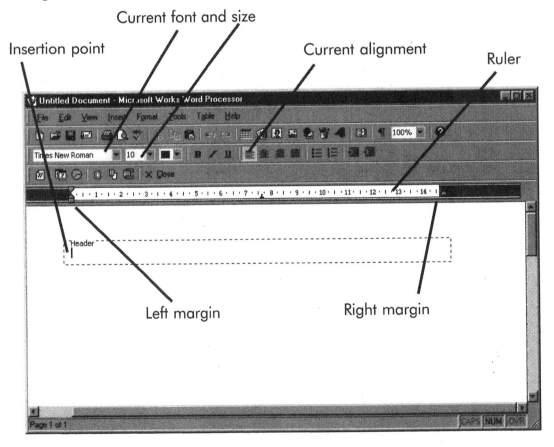

Insertion point

Current font and size

Current alignment

Ruler

Left margin

Right margin

Instant edits

❑ If you want to go back in the text, move the insertion point with the arrow keys or by pointing and clicking the mouse.

❑ If you spot any errors, [Backspace] erases to the left of the insertion point, [Delete] erases to the right.

❑ If you miss something out, move the insertion point back and type in the words. Existing text will normally (see below) shuffle up to make room for it.

Tip

Press [Insert] to switch into Overtype mode if you want to type over existing characters rather than insert new text amongst them.

Entering text

Don't think of the screen as a blank sheet of paper. You cannot start typing anywhere you like. The insertion point can only move where there is text or spaces. If you want to start over on the right, type spaces or tabs to push the insertion point across. If you want to start lower down on, press **[Enter]** to move the end of document marker down.

A word processor is not like a typewriter. When you reach the end of the line, just keep typing and let the automatic *wordwrap* function take the text on to the next line for you. Do not press **[Enter]** until you reach the end of a paragraph.

The advantage of wordwrap is that you can change the width between the margins, and the text will still flow smoothly from one line to the next.

[Enter] at the end of paragraphs only

Keep on typing when you reach here

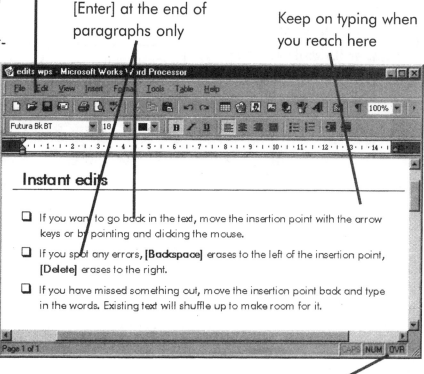

Insert/Overtype indicator

Selecting text

Text can be selected with the keys, but it is generally simplest to do it with the mouse. Once you have selected a block of text or a paragraph, you can:

- apply a font style or paragraph format – using the toolbar buttons or the Format menu. (See *Fonts*, page 32 and *Indents and Alignment*, page 42.)

- delete it – press **[Backspace]** or **[Delete]**;

- move it – see the Steps;

- get it into the Clipboard – see opposite.

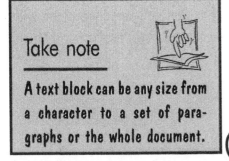

Take note

A text block can be any size from a character to a set of paragraphs or the whole document.

Basic steps

- ❑ To select a block

1 Place the insertion point at the start.

2 Hold down the left mouse button and drag to the end.

- ❑ To select a word

3 Double-click into the word.

- ❑ To select a sentence

4 Hold down [Ctrl].

5 Click anywhere within the sentence.

- ❑ To select all the text

6 Open the Edit menu and choose Select All.

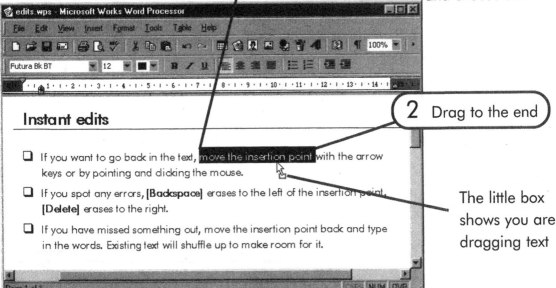

1 Click at the start

2 Drag to the end

Instant edits

❑ If you want to go back in the text, move the insertion point with the arrow keys or by pointing and clicking the mouse.

❑ If you spot any errors, **[Backspace]** erases to the left of the insertion point, **[Delete]** erases to the right.

❑ If you have missed something out, move the insertion point back and type in the words. Existing text will shuffle up to make room for it.

The little box shows you are dragging text

Basic steps

- [ ] To drag and drop selected text

1 Point anywhere within the selected block.

2 Hold down the left button and drag the insertion point. You will see a little box appear beneath beside the pointer.

3 Release the button to drop the text in at the insertion point.

- [ ] To copy text

1 Point anywhere within the selected block.

2 Hold down [Ctrl] while you drag.

3 Release the button to drop in the text.

Using the Clipboard

Dragging and dropping text can only be done within a document – and can only be done easily when you are not moving the block very far. To move a block over a distance, or from one document to another, you must use the **Edit** menu or toolbar buttons. Text can be cut or copied from your document into the Clipboard, and pasted wherever you want it. Learn the Control keystrokes for these commands – they are the same in all Windows applications.

- **Edit – Cut** [Ctrl]–[X] removes the original text, storing a copy in the Clipboard;

- **Edit – Copy** [Ctrl]–[C] copies the text into the Clipboard;

- **Edit – Paste** [Ctrl]–[V] inserts a copy of whatever is in the Clipboard.

These are on the Edit menu of all Windows applications

This will select the whole text

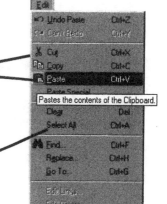

Take note

When you paste text from the Clipboard, it goes in after the insertion point or *replaces any text that is selected at the time.* Always check that nothing is highlighted, unless you do want to replace a block.

Take note

The Control key may be labelled either [Ctrl] or [Control].

Fonts

Font styles can be applied in two different ways.

● You can set them at the start, or at any point, to apply to everything you type afterwards – until you change them again.

● You can select a block, **anywhere in the middle of the text,** and apply a format to that block only.

All aspects of the appearance of text can be set through the **Format** menu, but if you are changing one feature only, it is often quicker to use the toolbar buttons or the keyboard shortcuts.

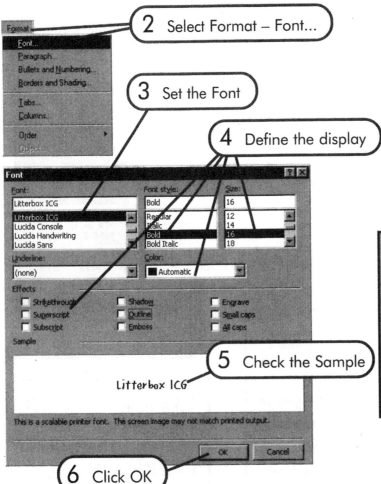

2 Select Format – Font...

3 Set the Font

4 Define the display

5 Check the Sample

6 Click OK

1 If you are formatting a block, select it first.

2 Open the Format menu and select Font...

3 At the dialog box, start by selecting a Font from the list.

4 Change the Size, Style, Color and Effects as required.

5 Check the appearance in the Sample pane, repeating steps 3 and 4 until you are happy with the results.

6 Click [OK] when you are done.

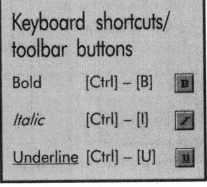

Keyboard shortcuts/ toolbar buttons

Bold	[Ctrl] – [B]	**B**
Italic	[Ctrl] – [I]	*I*
<u>Underline</u>	[Ctrl] – [U]	<u>U</u>

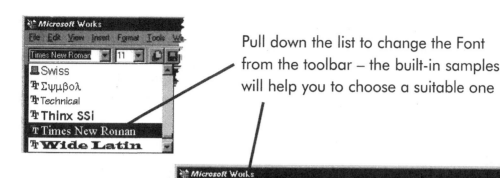

Pull down the list to change the Font from the toolbar – the built-in samples will help you to choose a suitable one

The font and style were changed when the insertion point was here – before typing in the text.

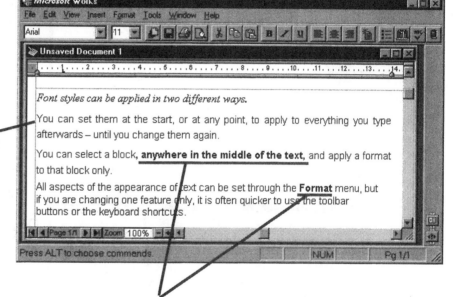

Font styles can be applied in two different ways.

You can set them at the start, or at any point, to apply to everything you type afterwards – until you change them again.

You can select a block, **anywhere in the middle of the text,** and apply a format to that block only.

All aspects of the appearance of text can be set through the **Format** menu, but if you are changing one feature only, it is often quicker to use the toolbar buttons or the keyboard shortcuts.

These blocks were selected, then formatted

Text sizes

9 point or less is for footnotes

12 point gives clear readable text

14 point works for sub-headings

18 point is good for titles

36 point makes a headline

Find and Replace

A simple **Find** will locate the next occurrence of a given word or phrase. You can use it to check documents for references to items, when you do not know if they are there or not. You can also use it to jump to a part of the document identified by a key word. The longer the document, the more useful this becomes.

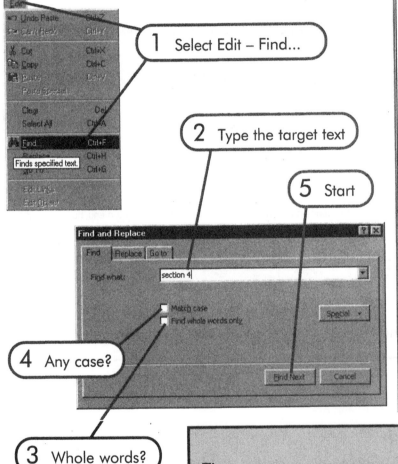

1 Select Edit – Find...

2 Type the target text

5 Start

4 Any case?

3 Whole words?

1 Open the Edit menu and select Find...

2 Type in the word or phrase to find.

3 If it might form part of a longer word, then check the Match Whole Word Only option.

4 If the pattern of capitals and lower case is important, check the Match Case option.

5 Click ▢Find Next to start the search.

6 If the text is present, it will be found and highlighted. You can then either look for the next occurrence, or Cancel to return to the document – at the site of the found text.

Tip

If you want to find or replace paragraph marks, tabs, non-breaking hyphens or other special characters, you can pick them from the list that drops down from the **Special** button.

Basic steps

1 Open the Edit menu and select Replace…

or

2 If the Find box is already open, click on the Replace tab.

3 Type in the word or phrase to find, and the replacement text.

4 Turn on the Match Whole Word Only and Match Case options if appropriate.

5 If you only want replace some of the occurrences, click `Find Next` to start, then `Replace` as needed.

6 For a clean sweep, click `Replace All` .

Tip

Before doing Replace All on a short word, turn on Find whole word only. There is a chance the word could be found as *part of* another.

Find and Replace will find the given text and replace it with a new phrase. It is said that some unscrupulous authors use this to make new books from old. A quick Replace on the names of the key characters and of the places, and you have a fresh novel!

It is more commonly used as a time-saver. If you had a long name, such as 'Butterworth-Heinemann', that had to be written several times in a document, you could type an abbreviation, 'B-H', and later use Replace to swap the full name back in.

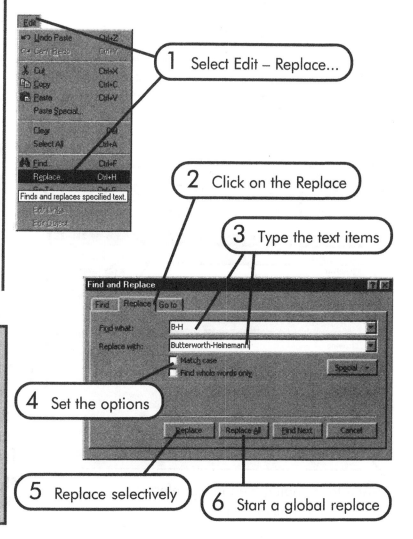

1 Select Edit – Replace…

2 Click on the Replace

3 Type the text items

4 Set the options

5 Replace selectively

6 Start a global replace

Spelling

Even the best spellers need these! You may not make spelling mistakes, but is your typing perfect?

The spelling checker works from a dictionary of over 100,000 words. It's a good number, but there will be some words that you use that are not present. Specialised terms and names of people and places are the most likely omissions. To cope with these, there is a user dictionary, to which you can add your own selection of words. Once added, they will be included in spelling checks in future.

The check can be run over a single, selected word, over a highlighted block, or throughout the document.

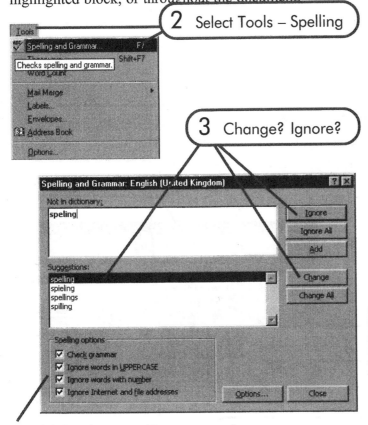

Useful for skipping filenames, references and technical stuff

1 If you only want to check one word, or a block, select it first.

2 Open the Tools menu and select Spelling and Grammar... or click .

3 When an unknown word is found, it is highlighted and the dialog box opens with these options:

Change Replace with a chosen Suggestion.

Change All Replace with this word every time.

Ignore It's OK, leave it...

Ignore All ... every time you see it

Add Add to your personal dictionary.

Take note

Turn on the **Check grammar** option if you want it to also check the structure and punctuation.

Basic steps

1 Select the word you would like to replace.

2 Open the Tools menu and select Thesaurus.

3 If the word can have several Meanings, select the closest from the list on the left.

4 Select a word from the Synonyms list on the right.

5 Click [Replace] to replace the word with the current synonym.

Thesaurus

Stuck for *le mot juste*? Let the Thesaurus suggest (offer, put forward, advise, recommend, advocate) a better (improved, enhanced, superior) word. With a bank of around 200,000 words to draw from, it can generally come up with something suitable (applicable, appropriate, apposite, apropos, germane, pertinent, relevant, to the point).

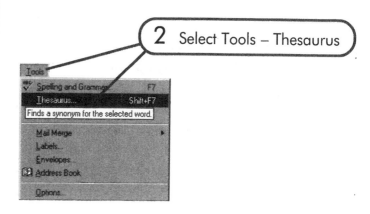

2 Select Tools – Thesaurus

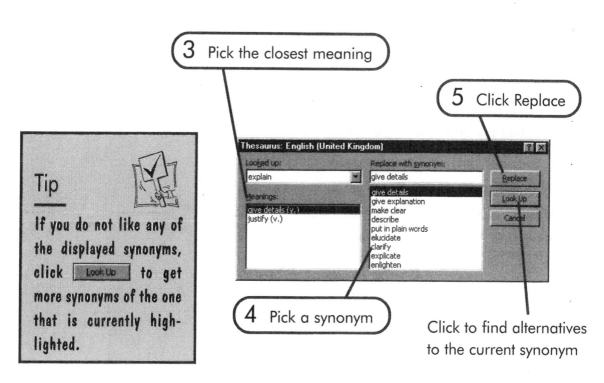

3 Pick the closest meaning

5 Click Replace

4 Pick a synonym

Click to find alternatives to the current synonym

Tip

If you do not like any of the displayed synonyms, click [Look Up] to get more synonyms of the one that is currently highlighted.

37

Summary

- ❑ When you start a new document, there are default settings for fonts and formats already in place. Change these at the start if you want a different appearance.

- ❑ The Insertion Point shows where text will appear when you type. Move it with the arrow keys or the mouse if you want to go back into your text to edit it.

- ❑ Corrections can be made as you type by pressing [Backspace], or left for tidying up later.

- ❑ A selected block of text can be formatted, deleted or moved to a new position.

- ❑ The Clipboard's Edit Cut and Paste facilities allow you to copy and move text between pages and between documents.

- ❑ You can easily set the font, size or style of selected blocks of text or of the whole document.

- ❑ Find will search documents for particular words, and can be used to jump to the location of a word.

- ❑ Replace lets you type in abbreviations, and replace them all at the end in a single operation.

- ❑ The Spelling checker is an invaluable aid for spotting mistypes, as well as spelling errors.

- ❑ The Thesaurus can help you to find the most appropriate words to express your meaning.

4 Working on layout

Page Setup

Before you get too far into typing the text, check that the basic layout of the page is right. Use the **Page Setup** routine to set the paper size, orientation and margins. And check the effect of these settings with **Print Preview**.

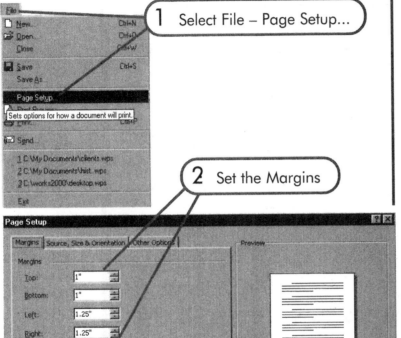

1 Select File – Page Setup...

2 Set the Margins

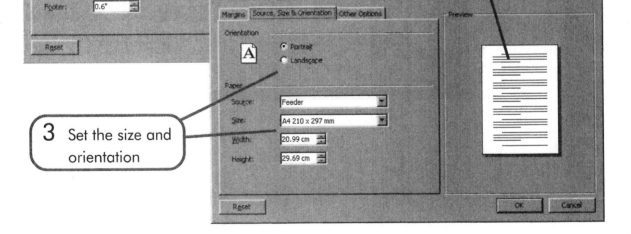

3 Set the size and orientation

1 From the File menu select Page Setup...

2 Set the Margins to suit – Header and Footer margins must be less than Top and Bottom margins.

3 Open the Source, Size & Orientation panel. Check the Paper size (normally A4 in the UK). Set the Orientation to *Landscape* if you want to print sideways.

4 Leave Other Options and click OK .

The Preview gives an idea of how a page will look

Basic steps

1 Open the File menu and select Print Preview... or click on the 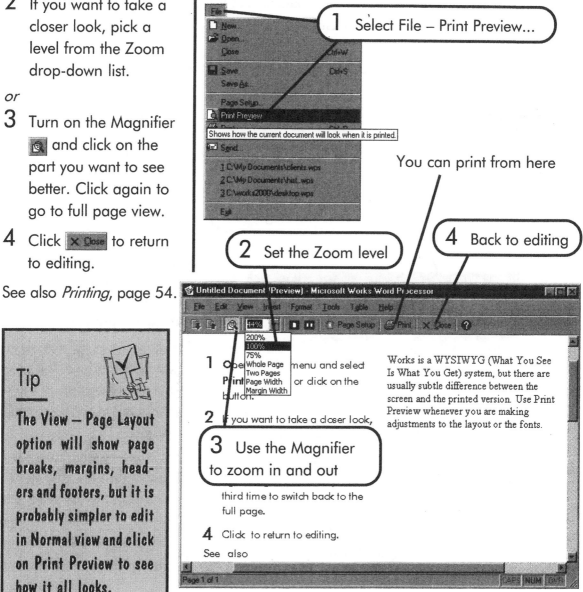 button.

2 If you want to take a closer look, pick a level from the Zoom drop-down list.

or

3 Turn on the Magnifier ⊞ and click on the part you want to see better. Click again to go to full page view.

4 Click ✕ Close to return to editing.

See also *Printing*, page 54.

See also *Printing*, page 54.

Tip

The View – Page Layout option will show page breaks, margins, headers and footers, but it is probably simpler to edit in Normal view and click on Print Preview to see how it all looks.

Print Preview

Works is a WYSIWYG (What You See Is What You Get) system, but there are usually subtle differences between the screen and the printed version. Use Print Preview whenever you are making adjustments to the layout or the fonts.

1 Select File – Print Preview...

Shows how the current document will look when it is printed.

You can print from here

2 Set the Zoom level

4 Back to editing

3 Use the Magnifier to zoom in and out

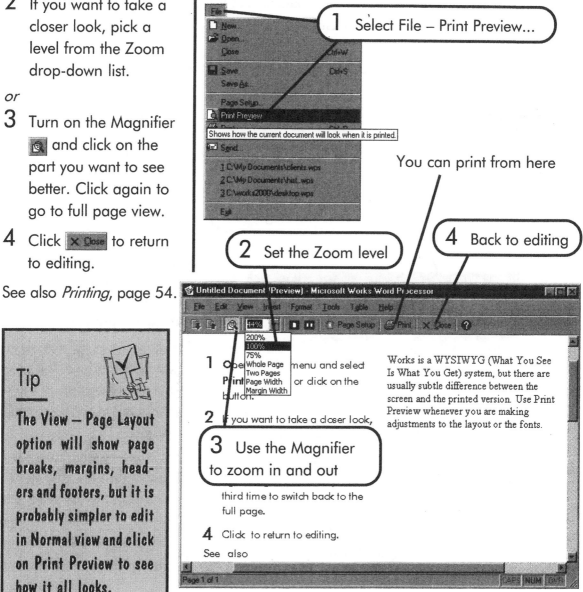

Untitled Document (Preview) - Microsoft Works Word Processor

200%
100%
75%
Whole Page
Two Pages
Page Width
Margin Width

1 Open the File menu and select Print Preview... or click on the button.

2 If you want to take a closer look,

third time to switch back to the full page.

4 Click to return to editing.

See also

Works is a WYSIWYG (What You See Is What You Get) system, but there are usually subtle difference between the screen and the printed version. Use Print Preview whenever you are making adjustments to the layout or the fonts.

Page 1 of 1

41

Indents and Alignment

The Paragaph... dialog box gives you a one-stop method of setting the layout of text – its alignment, indents from the margins and spacing between lines.

● Indents (pushing text in from the margins) can be set from the ruler, and alignments from toolbar buttons, but it is only in the box that you can set indents really accurately.

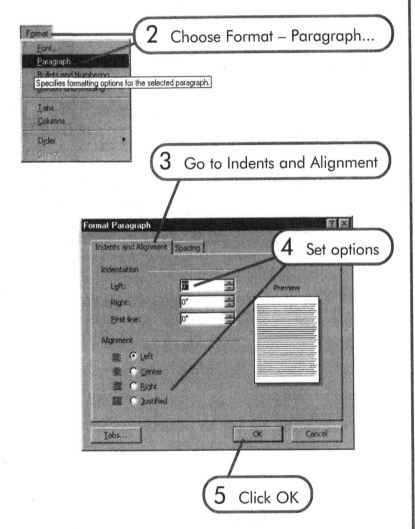

1 Select the paragraphs, or place the cursor to format new text.

2 Open the Format menu and select Paragraph...

3 At the Paragraph dialog box, switch to Indents and Alignment.

4 Set the options.

5 Click ⬚OK⬚ when you have done.

❑ Alignments

Left ▤ alignment is the default. Lines start flush on the left, but have ragged right edges.

Fully justified ▤ text aligns with both margins. This gives a crisp right edge, but can produce big gaps between words.

Centre ▤ alignment is good for titles, but does not make for easy reading.

Use Right ▤ alignment for addresses, dates and other headings.

Basic steps

Indents

1 If the Ruler is not visible, open the View menu and click on Ruler.

❑ To set the Right indent

Point anywhere on the right triangle and drag it into position.

❑ To set the Left indent

Point at the *lower* left triangle and drag.

❑ To set the First line indent

Point at the *upper* left triangle and drag.

The width of lines of text can be controlled by both Margins and Indents.

● **Margins** are printer settings and controlled by the Page Setup routines (see page 40).

● **Indents** push the text in further from the margins, and are used to pick out paragraphs, for emphasis.

Left and Right indents set the distance of all lines from the margins. This paragraph has a left indent of 1.5cm, and a right indent of 1cm.

First line indent sets the difference between the first and later lines. It can be negative – left of the left indent – to create a **hanging indent**, as here.

Indents can be set most accurately by typing values into the **Indents and Alignments** page of the **Paragraph** dialog box, but much of the time it is simpler to use the indent marker triangles on the ruler.

First line indent

Left indent

Right indent

Right margin

Left margin

The guide line appears as you drag on an indent marker

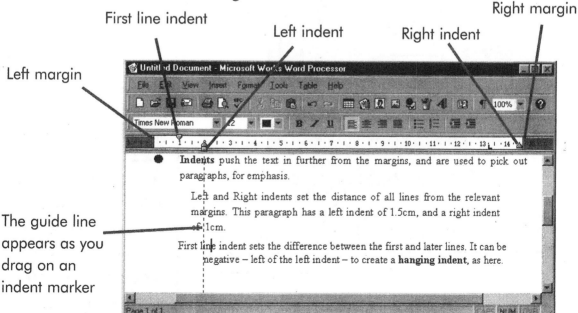

Spacing

The **line spacing** can be set to single, 1.5 lines, double, triple or quadruple. For most purposes, it is enough to be able to switch between single spacing and double spacing.

Double-spacing can be used for emphasis, though **bold**, *italics* or a larger font size will do that better. It is best kept for those times when you want to leave space between lines for people to write notes or corrections.

If you want to separate your paragraphs, or make a selected paragraph stand out from the rest, you can set the number (or the fraction) of lines **before** or **after** the text.

1 Select the paragraphs.

2 Open the Format – Paragraph dialog box, and switch to Spacing.

❑ To separate paragraphs

3 Use the arrows or type the number of lines Before or After (or both).

❑ To spread text within paragraphs

4 Select a Line spacing option from the drop-down list.

5 Click [OK] to exit.

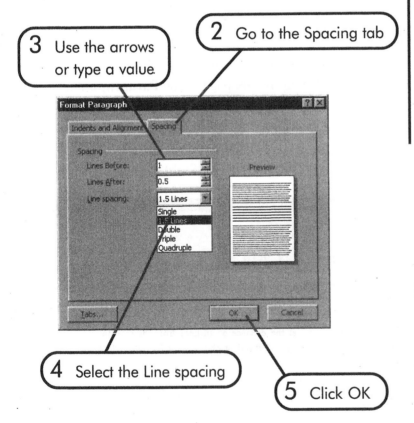

3 Use the arrows or type a value.

2 Go to the Spacing tab

4 Select the Line spacing

5 Click OK

Tip

If you have a set of bullet points or similar items and want to space them out for extra clarity, use a *Before* or *After* option not *Line spacing*.

Basic steps

1 Select the block in which you want tabs.

2 From the Format menu select Tabs...

3 Pick the tab and set its alignment and leader.

4 Click **Set** to store its settings.

5 Repeat 3 and 4 for other tabs then click **OK**.

❑ To remove unwanted tabs, drag them down off the ruler, or use the **Clear** button.

Setting left tabs is simple – just click on the ruler. For centre, right and decimal tabs you must either bring their buttons onto the toolbar, or use the Tabs... dialog box. This is also used for setting leader dots or lines.

Centre	Left	Right	Decimal
WT1	Widget, large....... 94		7.99
WT2	Widget, small 15		3.99
GD	Gadget 44		11.49
GMB3	Gimble 5		1,029.99

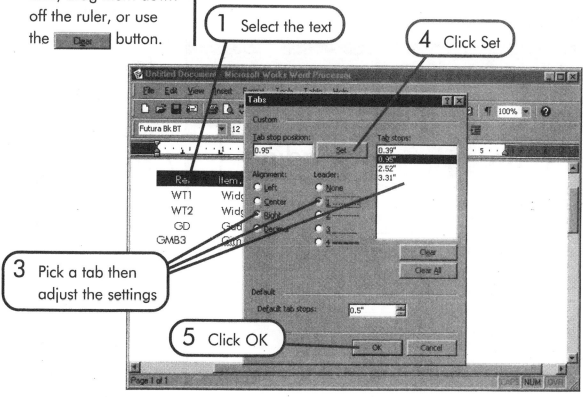

1 Select the text

4 Click Set

3 Pick a tab then adjust the settings

5 Click OK

Borders and Shading

If you want to place lines anywhere around a block of text, or add decorative borders around the whole page, use **Format – Borders and Shading...**

Use lines above or below paragraphs to mark off sections.

> Lines on either side can help to emphasise a block of text.

Lines all around create a solid box. This can work well around the title on the front page of a report.

Used sparingly, light or brightly coloured backgrounds will focus the reader's attention onto selected items – but too much just creates confusion!

- ❏ Text borders
1 Select the paragraphs to be bordered.
2 Open the Format menu and select Borders and Shading...
3 Set the Line Style, and Color.
4 If you do not want a border all round, click on the sides to have lines.
- ❏ Page borders
5 In Apply to: switch to Page.
6 Select a Border Art style and adjust its Width if required.
7 Click ▭OK▭.

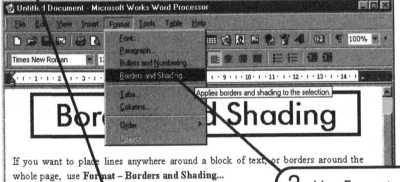

1 Select the paragraph

2 Use Format – Borders and Shading...

3 Set the style and colour

4 Which sides?

Tip

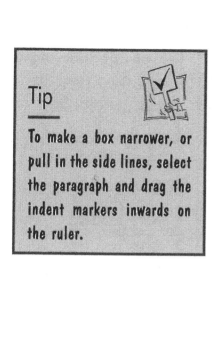

To make a box narrower, or pull in the side lines, select the paragraph and drag the indent markers inwards on the ruler.

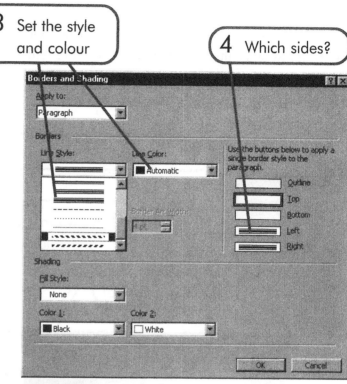

Borders and Shading

Apply to:

Paragraph

Borders

Line Style:

Line Color:

Automatic

Border Art Width:

Shading

Fill Style:

None

Color 1:

Black

Color 2:

White

Use the buttons below to apply a single border style to the paragraph.

Outline

Top

Bottom

Left

Right

OK   Cancel

5 Switch to Page

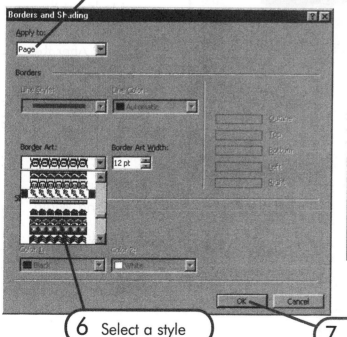

Borders and Shading

Apply to:

Page

Borders

Line Style:

Line Color:

Automatic

Border Art:

Border Art Width:

12 pt

Outline

Top

Bottom

Left

Right

Color 1:

Black

Color 2:

White

OK   Cancel

Take note

Shading is handled much the same as Borders. You may find it best to select the pattern first.

With strongly-coloured shading, set a contrasting colour for the text.

6 Select a style

7 Click OK

Tables

If you have a set of figues or other data that you want to lay out in a neat row and column format, you can do this with tabs, but it's simpler to use a table – you don't have to fiddle around with tab settings and there are ready-made formats to give you a good-looking result.

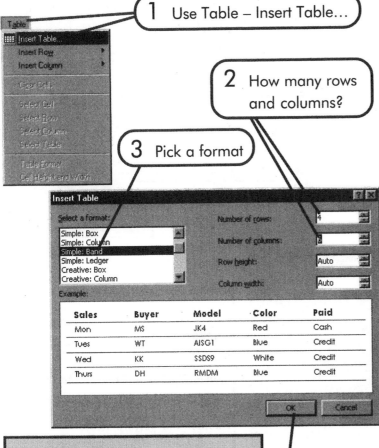

1 Use Table – Insert Table...

2 How many rows and columns?

3 Pick a format

4 Click OK

Table formats

'Box' gives a simple outline;
'Column' draws lines between columns;
'Band' draws lines between the rows;
'Ledger' colours alternate rows.

1 Open the Table menu and select Insert Table... or click .

2 Set the number of rows and columns.

3 Select a format.

4 Click OK.

5 Enter your data, pressing [Tab] to move from one cell to the next.

❑ To add a row or column

6 Open the Table menu, point to Insert Row (Column) then choose Before or After the current one.

❑ To adjust the size of cells

7 Select the cells.

8 Use Table – Cell Height and Width.

9 Set the Height and Width and click OK.

5 Enter the data

6 Insert a row or column?

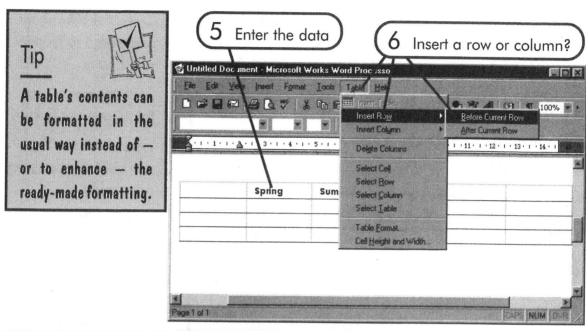

7 Select the cells

8 Use Table – Cell Height and Width

9 Set the Height and Width

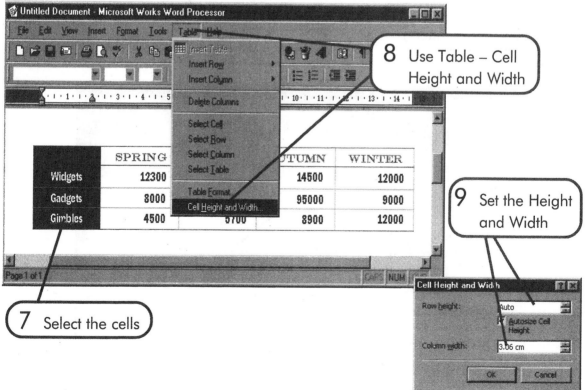

Headers and footers

Headers and footers , if defined, will appear at the top and bottom of every page. You can write into them the report title, chapter heading or author, and insert the current date and time, the page number and file name. These insertions are managed and kept up to date by Works.

You can use the normal range of formatting and alignment on headers and footers.

1 Open the View menu and switch to Header and Footer.

2 Click the cursor into the Header or Footer.

3 Type in the text that you want to appear on each page.

   Inserting items

4 Place the cursor where the item is to go.

5 Click 🔢 to add the date, or access it through the Insert menu.

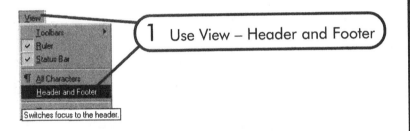

1 Use View – Header and Footer

2 Click into Header

5 Select item to insert

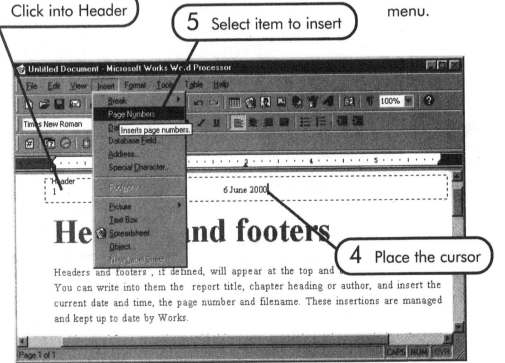

4 Place the cursor

50

6 With Date and Time, choose a format in the dialog box, then click ▮ Insert ▮.

7 Select and format the header/footer as required.

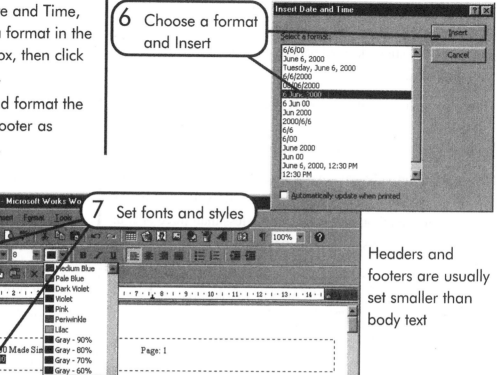

6 Choose a format and Insert

Insert Date and Time

Select a format:

- 6/6/00
- June 6, 2000
- Tuesday, June 6, 2000
- 6/6/2000
- 06/06/2000
- 6 June, 2000
- 6 Jun 00
- Jun 2000
- 2000/6/6
- 6/6
- 6/00
- June 2000
- Jun 00
- June 6, 2000, 12:30 PM
- 12:30 PM

Insert Cancel

☐ Automatically update when printed

7 Set fonts and styles

Headers and footers are usually set smaller than body text

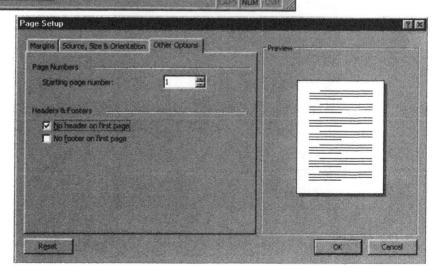

If you don't want Headers or Footers on the first (title?) page, go to Page Setup, and on the Other Options tab turn on the No header (footer) on first page option

Columns

Use a multiple column layout where you want to have a number of separate stories on a page, or where a report is broken down into a set of distinct, headed paragraphs, perhaps interspersed with graphics.

Short paragraphs, that cover only a couple of lines across the full width of the page, will take 6 or 8 lines in columns. These solid blocks of text look more balanced and are easier to read.

You would normally want two or three columns on an A4 page – with four or more, the columns are too narrow, unless you are using a very small point size. Anything less than three or four words to a line looks far too scrappy.

1 Open the Format menu and select Columns...

2 At the dialog box, set the Number of columns and the Space between them.

3 Check Lines between if you want them. These will not be visible during editing, but are applied at print time.

4 Click OK .

5 Start typing and leave Works to flow the text into the columns.

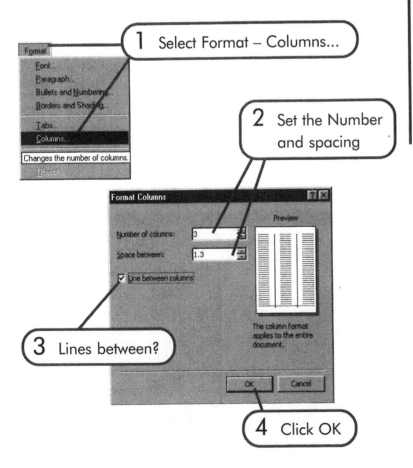

1 Select Format – Columns...

2 Set the Number and spacing

3 Lines between?

4 Click OK

Take note

The same column format applies to all the pages in the document.

Text can only be written inside the columns, but if you want headlines across the page, insert WordArt text. At first, this will be squeezed into a single column. To spread it across the columns use the *Absolute* Text Wrap setting. (See *WordArt*, page 126.)

Short items can be picked out by dropping a border round them. This does not work as well in a full-width layout.

Short paragraphs work better in columns

Columns

Where?

Use a multiple column layout where you want to have a number of separate stories on a page, or where a report is broken down into a set of distinct, headed paragraphs, perhaps interspersed with graphics.

Chunkier text

Short paragraphs, that cover only a couple of lines across the full width of the page, will take 6 or 8 lines in columns. These solid blocks of text look more balanced and are easier to read.

Flexibility

With a three-column page, you have flexibility in placing graphics. Small ones can fit in one column, while larger ones can be spread over two or three.

Boxed items

Short items can be picked out by dropping a border round them. This does not work as well in a full-width layout.

How?

Simple. Just select the Column format and tell Works how many columns you want on a page. You want two or three columns on an A4 page. With four, the columns are too narrow, unless you are using a very small point size. Anything less than three or four words to a line looks far too scrappy.

Headlines

Text can only be written inside columns, but if you want headlines across the page, you can insert Word Art. (See *Word Art*).

All the Same

If you decide to use columns, the format applies to every page in the document.

Columns **Columns**

Short paragraphs work better in columns

WordArt can also be used for captions across the columns

With a three-column page, you have flexibility in placing graphics. Small ones can fit in one column, while larger ones can be spread over two or three.

Printing

The Print Preview will give you a good idea of how documents will appear, but you can never be entirely sure until you see the printed copy. Some fonts do not come out quite the same on paper as on screen; grey shades become dot patterns; colours are never quite the same. If you have a long document, it is often worth printing a couple of sample pages, and checking those, before committing the whole lot to paper.

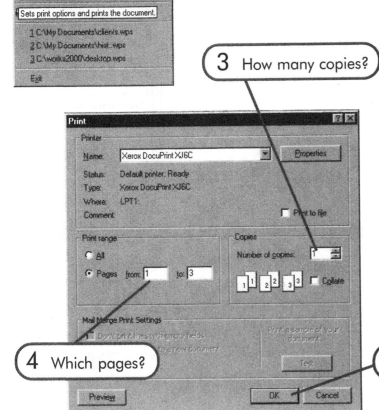

2 Select File – Print...

3 How many copies?

4 Which pages?

5 Click OK

☐ Quick printing

1 If you don't want to change any of the current print settings, just click 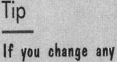 on the toolbar.

☐ Controlled printing

2 Open the File menu and select Print...

3 Set the Number of Copies.

4 Set the Page Range, specifying Start and End pages, or All.

5 Click [OK].

Tip

If you change any settings, use the Preview option to check their effect before sending the file to the printer.

54

Basic steps

1 Open the File menu and select Print...

2 If you are switching to another printer, select it from the Name list.

3 If you want to adjust the print settings, click `Properties...`.

❑ Every printer has its own Properties dialog box – the one below is for a Xerox inkjet – but all give you some control over the quality of printed output. Investigate the properties of your printer.

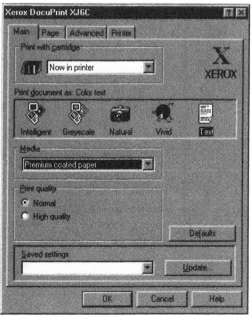

Printer properties

Works runs through Windows, and the printer setup routines that you will have done there, will be in place for your Works printing. As a result, you will probably find that you only have to bother with this on rare occasions. Go to the printer's Properties panel if you want to switch print sideways, or adjust the quality of the print.

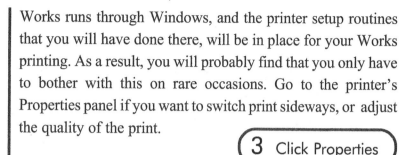

3 Click Properties

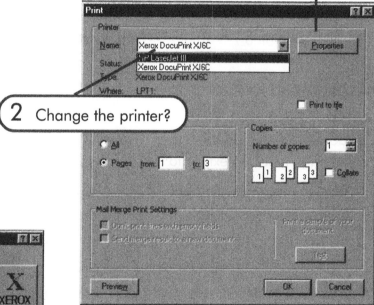

2 Change the printer?

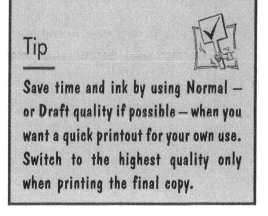

Tip

Save time and ink by using Normal – or Draft quality if possible – when you want a quick printout for your own use. Switch to the highest quality only when printing the final copy.

Summary

- [ ] Use the Page Setup routines to set the paper size, orientation and margins.

- [ ] Use Print Preview to check the appearance of documents before printing.

- [ ] Indents, Alignment and Tabs can be set from the ruler or toolbar buttons, though you may have to use the dialog boxes to get fine control.

- [ ] Tabs are easily set via the Ruler, but for more accurate positioning you should use the Format Tabs dialog box.

- [ ] You can set the Spacing between lines and between paragraphs.

- [ ] Borders can be added to any or all of the edges of a selected block of text, or to the whole page.

- [ ] You can use patterned and coloured Shading to highlight blocks of text.

- [ ] Tables are the simplest and neatest way to present columns and rows of figures and other data.

- [ ] Headers and Footers can be added. You can insert into them the page number, filename and date, if wanted.

- [ ] Multiple columns offer a number of advantages for newsletters and certain types of reports.

- [ ] Check the settings before printing. If required, you can adjust them in the printer's Properties dialog box.

5 Working with numbers

Cells and contents

A spreadsheet is a grid of cells into which text, numbers and formulae can be written. With the Works spreadsheet, you also have control of fonts, lines and background patterns to enhance the appearance, so that, for example, the spreadsheet that calculates the bills can also produce professional-looking invoices. Where the spreadsheet is being used to analyse cash flows, departmental budgets or other sets of values that change over time or category, the easy chart-drawing routines can make the patterns of change more visible.

Two layers

With a word processor document, what you see is what you get. Spreadsheets are different. The text, numbers and formulae that are held in the cells are not necessarily what you see on screen. With formulae, the results are displayed; text items that are longer than the width of the cell will be clipped short if there is something in the cell to the right; numbers will appear as a set of # if they are too large to fit in a cell.

Entering and editing data

Entering data into a spreadsheet is significantly different from entering it into a word processor. Everything goes in through the Formula line, where the system checks it to see if it is a piece of text, a number or a formula – for these are each treated differently. The Formula line is linked to the current cell. It displays whatever is in the cell at the moment, and anything entered into the formula line is transferred to the cell.

❑ To enter data

1 Point at the target cell and click on it to make it current.

2 Start to type. The characters will appear in the formula line.

3 Use the [Left] / [Right] arrow keys to move along the line; [Backspace] or [Delete] to erase errors.

4 Click ☑ or press [Enter] when you have done. The display version of the data will appear in the cell.

❑ To edit cell contents

1 Make the target cell current.

2 Click in the Formula line, or press [F2] to start editing.

3 Click ☑ or press [Enter] to accept the changes. Click ☒ or press [Escape] to abandon.

Jargon

Current cell – the last one you clicked with the mouse. It is marked by double-line borders.

Cell reference – a Column letter/Row number combination that identifies a cell. In the diagram, the current cell is C8 (Column C, Row 8).

Range – a set of cells, which may be one or more full rows or columns, or a block somewhere in the middle of the sheet.

Formula line – the slot at the top. Its contents are transferred to the current cell when you press [Enter]. All data is entered into cells through this line.

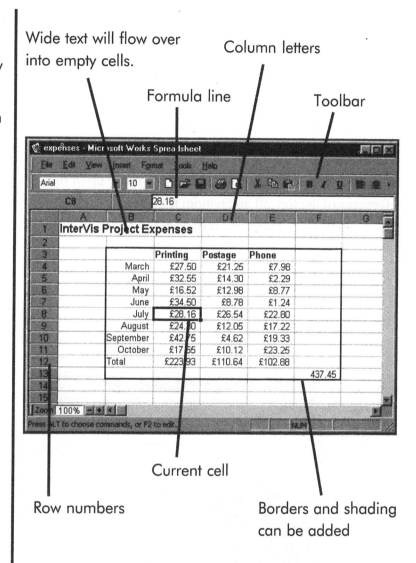

Wide text will flow over into empty cells.

Column letters

Formula line

Toolbar

Current cell

Row numbers

Borders and shading can be added

Take note

Works spreadsheet has 256 columns and 16,384 rows — that's a total of 4,194,304 cells! Big enough for you?

Selecting cells

Once you have selected a cell, or a range of cells, you can:

- apply a font style or alignment;
- add a border to some or all of its edges;
- erase its contents;
- use its references in a formula;
- move it to another position.

If you have to type a range reference, it is made up of the cell references of the top left and bottom right corners. Most of the time you will be able to get the references by selecting the range with the mouse.

Block references shown here

1 Start here

2 Drag to the opposite corner

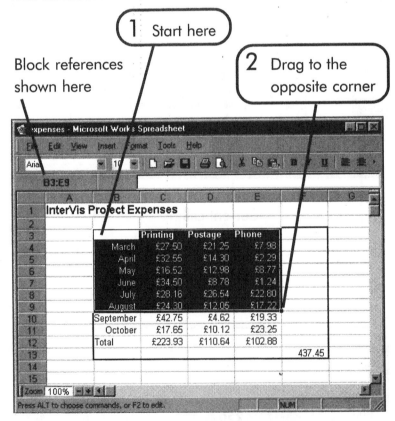

Basic steps

❑ To select a block

1 Point to the top left cell (or any corner).

2 Hold down the mouse button and drag the highlight over the block.

❑ To select a set of rows

3 Point to the row number at the top or bottom of the set.

4 Drag up or down over the numbers to high-light the rows you want.

Tip

In a selected range, all the cells will be shown in reverse colour, except for the first one — the current cell. It's easy to think that this one hasn't been selected. Don't be misled.

❏ To select a set of columns

1 Point to the column letter at one end of the set.

2 Drag across the top of the columns to include the ones you want.

❏ To select all cells

3 Click on the top left corner, where the row and column headers meet.

Or

4 Open the Edit menu and choose Select All.

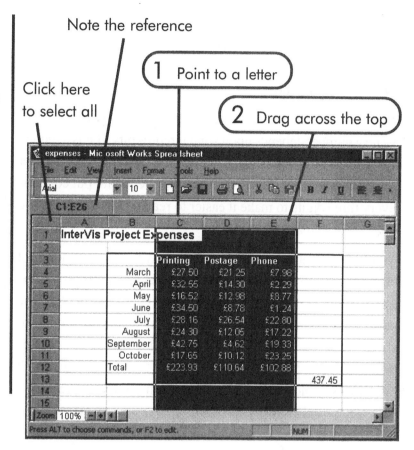

Note the reference

Click here to select all

1 Point to a letter

2 Drag across the top

These select the row or column of the current cell – clicking is quicker!

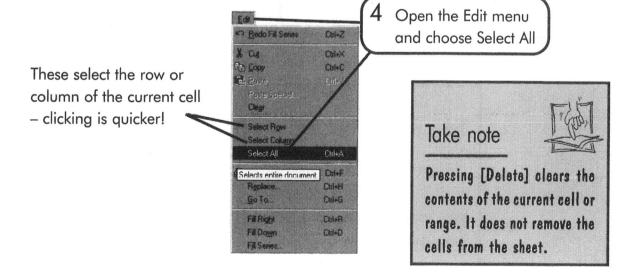

4 Open the Edit menu and choose Select All

Fonts and formats

Setting font types, styles and sizes for text is exactly the same here as it is in the word processor. Just select the block to be restyled and click a toolbar button or use the **Format – Font and Style** dialog box.

Number formats are a different matter. The way in which we write a number depends upon what it represents. If it is a money value, we would write a £ sign before and show two figures after the decimal point; with a large number, we would put commas every three digits to make it easier to read; if it is a percent, we place a % sign after it.

Works knows about all this. It can display numbers in different formats, and can understand numbers that are written in different formats. Type in £12,345.67 and it will realise that the underlying number is 12345.67, and also that you want to display it as currency. Type in 50% and it will store it as 0.5, while showing 50% on screen. Type in 0181-123 4567 and it will not be fooled into thinking its a sum – this gets treated as text. Try it and see for yourself.

Basic steps

1 Select the range of cells to be formatted.

2 Open the Format menu and select Number...

3 Select a Format from the panel on the left.

4 Set the number of decimal places.

5 With *Currency* values, you may want to use the Negative numbers in red option.

6 Check the Sample and adjust the options as required.

7 Click ⌷ OK ⌷.

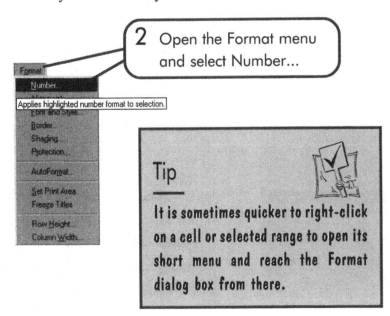

2 Open the Format menu and select Number...

Format
Number...
Applies highlighted number format to selection.
Font and Style...
Border...
Shading...
Protection...
AutoFormat...
Set Print Area
Freeze Titles
Row Height...
Column Width...

Tip

It is sometimes quicker to right-click on a cell or selected range to open its short menu and reach the Format dialog box from there.

Take note

There's a **Currency** format button on the toolbar and you can add buttons for the **Percent** and **Comma** formats — see page 76.

General displays numbers as they were written.

Currency 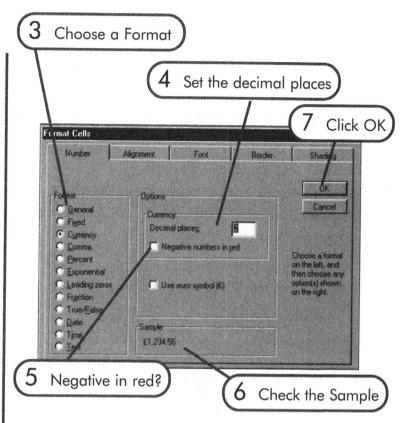 places a £ (or other currency sign) at the front, and commas every 3 digits.

Commas places a comma every 3 digits.

Percent turns a fraction value into a percentage.

Exponential is used for very large or very small numbers.

Fractions can sometimes be useful. Let it work out the closest fraction, or fix the denominator.

Text treats the digits as text, not as a value.

3 Choose a Format

4 Set the decimal places

7 Click OK

Format Cells

Number | Alignment | Font | Border | Shading

Format
- General
- Fixed
- Currency
- Comma
- Percent
- Exponential
- Leading zeros
- Fraction
- True/False
- Date
- Time
- Text

Options

Currency
Decimal places: 2

☐ Negative numbers in red

☐ Use euro symbol (€)

Sample
£1,234.56

OK
Cancel

Choose a format on the left, and then choose any option(s) shown on the right.

5 Negative in red?

6 Check the Sample

This screenshot shows a small selection of the number formats that Works offers. The number of decimal places can be set in any format. With Currency and Comma, you can have negative values shown in red.

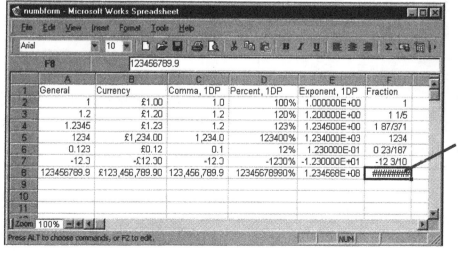

	A	B	C	D	E	F
1	General	Currency	Comma, 1DP	Percent, 1DP	Exponent, 1DP	Fraction
2	1	£1.00	1.0	100%	1.000000E+00	1
3	1.2	£1.20	1.2	120%	1.200000E+00	1 1/5
4	1.2345	£1.23	1.2	123%	1.234500E+00	1 87/371
5	1234	£1,234.00	1,234.0	123400%	1.234000E+03	1234
6	0.123	£0.12	0.1	12%	1.230000E-01	0 23/187
7	-12.3	-£12.30	-12.3	-1230%	-1.230000E+01	-12 3/10
8	123456789.9	£123,456,789.90	123,456,789.9	12345678990%	1.234568E+08	########

If you see ######, widen the column to display the number in full.

Alignment

There are more alignment options in the Spreadsheet than in the Word Processor.

Left, **Right** and **Centre** alternatives, which can be used to align text within cells, are available on the toolbar ▤▤▤.

The **Format – Alignment** panel has vertical options allowing you to place the text at the top, bottom or middle of cells, plus other *horizontal* options, **General**, **Fill** and **Center across selection**, and a **Wrap text** option.

● **General** is the default setting. It aligns text to the left and numbers to the right, and for most purposes this is the best way to display them.

1 Select the range of cells to be aligned.

2 Open the Format menu and select Alignment...

3 Select a Horizontal Alignment option.

4 If you want to adjust the Vertical position of the text within the cell, set an option.

5 Click ◾OK◾.

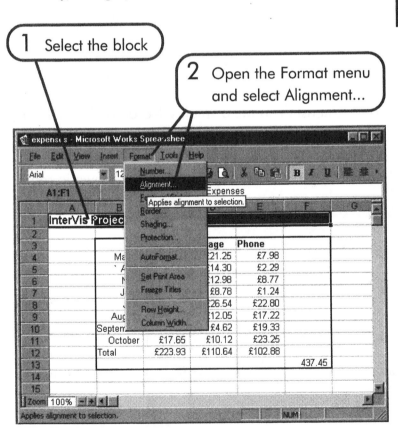

1 Select the block

2 Open the Format menu and select Alignment...

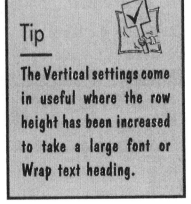

Tip

The Vertical settings come in useful where the row height has been increased to take a large font or Wrap text heading.

General aligns text to the left and numbers to the right.

Left, Right and Centre are the same as in the Word Processor.

Fill repeats whatever is in the first cell to fill the selected block. Use it to create dividing lines of characters.

Center across selection takes whatever is in the first cell and positions it centrally in the selected block.

Wrap text takes a long string of text and breaks it into multiple lines, to fit within the width of the cell. The row height will be increased to fit in the extra lines.

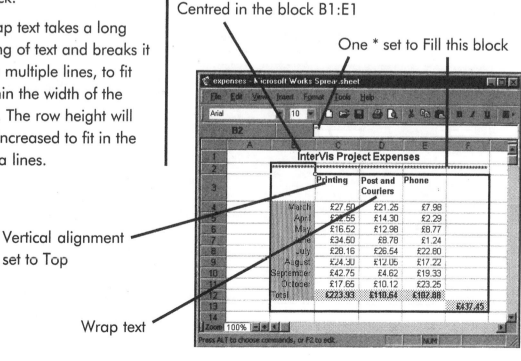

③ Set the alignment

⑤ Click OK

④ Set the Vertical position?

Centred in the block B1:E1

One * set to Fill this block

Vertical alignment set to Top

Wrap text

Borders and Shading

Borders can help to create a more visual structure to your sheet. Placed around a block, they will group the contents into one unit; placed along one side or beneath, they will separate values from their headings or totals.

Shaded and coloured backgrounds can focus your readers' attention on the most important aspects of the sheet – though some patterns can make the contents virtually unreadable. This may, or may not, be a bad thing.

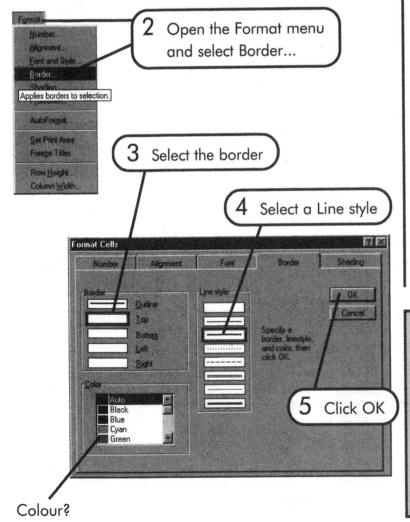

Colour?

❑ To add borders

1 Highlight the cells to be formatted.

2 Open the Format menu and select Border...

3 Click on the Borders which are to have lines.

4 Select the Line Style, and Color if wanted.

5 Click [OK].

❑ To remove borders

6 Highlight the cells to be tidied up.

7 Select the blank for the Line Style.

8 Click on the Borders that you want to clear.

Take note

Bug warning! Setting the Outline to blank does not remove lines. Set blanks for Top, Bottom. Left and Right to remove them all.

Basic steps

❏ To use shading

1 Highlight the cells to be formatted.

2 Open the Format menu and select Shading...

3 Pick a Pattern from the list.

4 Set Foreground and Background colours.

5 Check the Sample, and if you are happy, click [OK].

For coloured text, use the Color option in the Font and Style dialog box

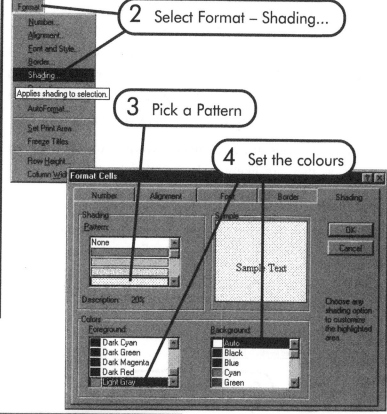

> **2** Select Format – Shading...

> **3** Pick a Pattern

> **4** Set the colours

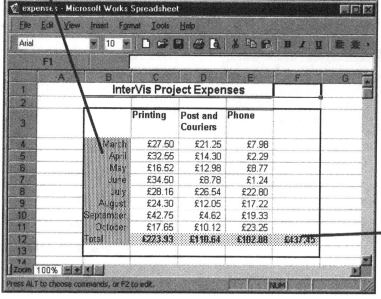

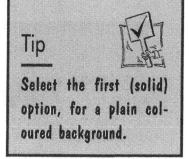

Tip

Select the first (solid) option, for a plain coloured background.

Patterns can make the contents unreadable

Autoformats

The spreadsheet's Autoformats, like the word processor's Easy Formats, offer an instant design solution for common situations. They are all based on headed tables or lists, but with 14 alternatives to choose from, you should find something there to suit most of your needs. The formatting includes that of the numbers, and the style of text, as well as shading and borders.

Colours and shades are best avoided if you are not using a colour printer, as they are likely to be translated into dot patterns, making text difficult to read.

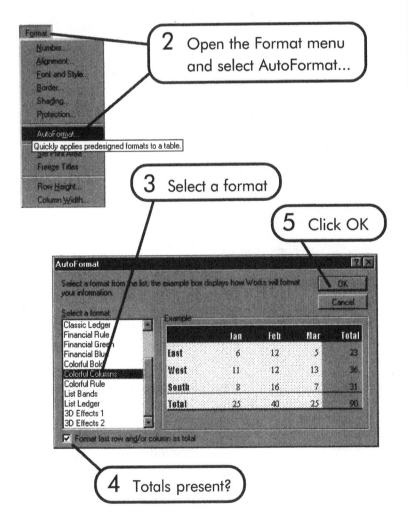

2 Open the Format menu and select AutoFormat...

3 Select a format

5 Click OK

4 Totals present?

1 Select the table or list to be formatted, including its headers and totals.

2 From the Format menu select AutoFormat...

3 Pick a format, checking its appearance with the Example.

4 If it is not appropriate, turn off Format last row and/or column as total.

5 Click [OK].

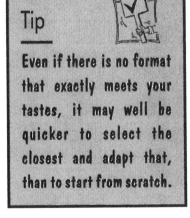

Tip

Even if there is no format that exactly meets your tastes, it may well be quicker to select the closest and adapt that, than to start from scratch.

Basic steps

❑ To total a range

1 Click on the cell below the column (or to the right of the row).

2 Click on the Σ *Autosum* button.

3 You will see that the column (or row) is highlighted, and that there is =SUM(*range*) in the formula line.

4 If range covers the right cells, click ✓ or press [Enter] to accept the formula.

You won't get far with a spreadsheet without writing formulae, but at least Works makes it a fairly painless business. If you just want to total a column or row of figures, it only takes a click of a button with **Autosum**. Other calculations take a little more effort, but point and click references, and readily-accessible lists of functions simplify the process and reduce the chance of errors.

A formula starts with the = sign and can contain a mixture of cell or range references, numbers, text and functions, joined by operators. These include the arithmetic symbols / * - + ^ and a few others.

Examples of simple formulae:

= 4 * C1   4 times the contents of cell C1

= B3+B4   the value in B3 added to that in B4

=SUM(A5:A12)the sum of the values in cells A5 to A12.

References can be typed into the formula line, or pulled in by clicking on a cell or highlighting a range.

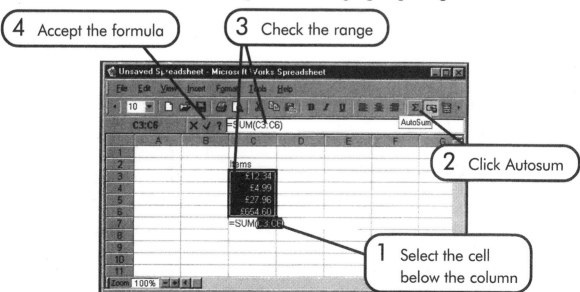

4 Accept the formula

3 Check the range

2 Click Autosum

1 Select the cell below the column

3 Number or reference

4 Type an operator

2 Type =

5 Number or reference

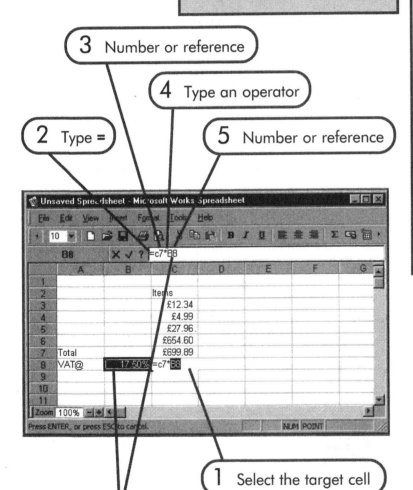

1 Select the target cell

When Works expects a reference, clicking on a cell writes the reference into the formula

☐ To write a formula

1 Click on the cell where the formula is to go.

2 Type =

3 Type the number, or point and click to get a cell reference.

4 Type an operator symbol **/ * - +**

5 Type the next number, or select the next reference.

6 Repeat steps 4 and 5, as necessary, to complete the formula.

7 Click ☑ or press [Enter].

Tip

If a cell displays the formula, not its result, there is an error in it. Select the cell and press [F2] to edit it.

Basic steps

- ❑ To name a range
1 Select the cell or the range.
2 Open the Insert menu and select Range Name..
3 Type a suitable name into the top slot.
4 Click [OK].
- ❑ To remove a name
5 Open the Insert menu and select Range Name...
6 Highlight the name in the list.
7 Click [Delete].

Using names

Cell and range references are hard to remember, and if you reorganise the layout of the spreadsheet, you may have to learn them all again. To make life simpler, Works allows you to give meaningful names to cells and ranges. Use them. They will make your formulae more readable, and if you want to transfer data into a word processed document, you can only do this with named ranges.

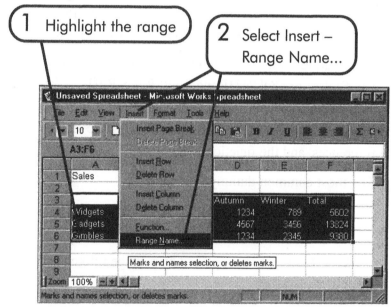

1 Highlight the range

2 Select Insert – Range Name...

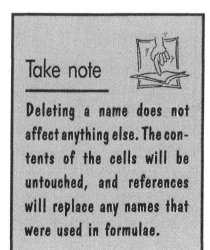
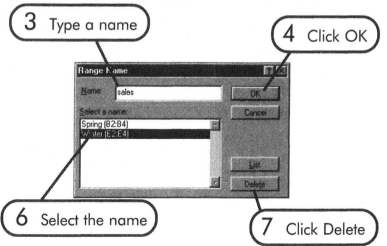

3 Type a name

4 Click OK

6 Select the name

7 Click Delete

Functions

A function takes one or more number or text values, performs some kind of process on them and gives a new value in return. It may be a simple process, as with SUM, which adds up a range of numbers. It may be a familiar one such as SIN, which gives the sine of an angle. It may be a complex process that you wouldn't meet anywhere except on a spreadsheet. PMT, for example, will give you the regular repayment on a mortgage. There is no room here to look at these functions properly, but what we can do is cover the basics of how to use them.

All functions come with dummy arguments in their brackets, e.g. SIN(x) or COUNT(RangeRef0,RangeRef1,...). These tell you the type of values that you should be supplying to the function. Replace the dummies with suitable cell or range references, and the function is ready to roll.

The most common dummy arguments are:

x standing for a number or the reference of a cell that contains a number

RangeRef0   to be replaced by a range reference

...   indicates that you can repeat the last type of value. For example, COUNT(RangeRef0,RangeRef1,...) tells you how many cells in one or more ranges contain something. It could be written:

COUNT(A2:A12)   for one partial column

COUNT(A1:E12)   for one block

COUNT(A2:A12, E5:H10)   counting two ranges.

Basic steps

1 Select the cell into which the formula should go.

2 Open the Insert menu and select Function... or click the Insert Function button, if you have added it to your toolbar.

3 Pick the Category of function from the panel on the left.

4 Scroll through the list to find the one you want, and click on it.

5 Click [Insert] to copy it to the formula line.

6 Replace the dummy argument(s) with suitable values or references.

7 Click ☑ or press [Enter] to accept the formula.

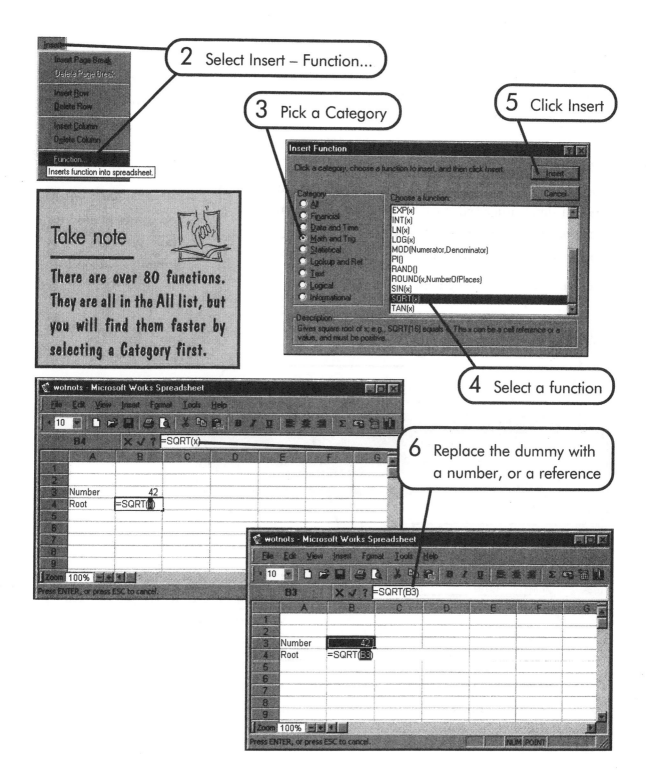

2 Select Insert – Function...

3 Pick a Category

5 Click Insert

Take note

There are over 80 functions. They are all in the All list, but you will find them faster by selecting a Category first.

4 Select a function

6 Replace the dummy with a number, or a reference

Lookup functions

One category of functions that are worth exploration are the Lookup functions. They can be really useful, and in getting to grips with these you will master most of the techniques you need for working with other functions.

A Lookup function will scan through a list of items in a table, to find a key item, then pick a value out of the corresponding place in another list within the table. The example opposite shows a simple price and stock list being used by two Lookup formulae. When an item's name is typed into a key cell, the functions scan the list and pick out its price and stock level.

There are two similar functions.

Basic steps

❑ To use VLOOKUP

1 Create a table of data, with index values – the keywords or reference numbers – on the left.

2 Pick a cell into which you will write the key value and type in something which is in the table. This will test the formulae.

3 Select the cell which will hold the formula.

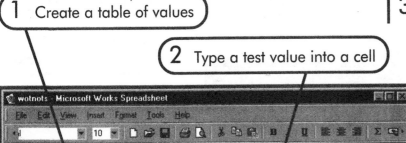

1 Create a table of values

2 Type a test value into a cell

3 Go to the formula's cell

The key items – the ones to be matched by the Lookup function – must be in the first column. The values to be looked up are in columns to its right.

4 Call up the Insert Function... dialog box.

5 Click on the Lookup and Ref category, select VLOOKUP.

6 Click [Insert] to copy it into the formula line.

7 The *LookupValue* will be highlighted. Select the cell containing your key value to replace this dummy with the reference.

8 Highlight *RangeRef*, then select the range that covers the table.

9 Delete *ColNum* and type 1 to get the value from the first column to the right of the index values, or 2 to get the value in the second column.

10 Click [✓] to accept the formula.

● **HLOOKUP** works with tables where the index values are written across the top of the table;

● **VLOOKUP** expects the index values to be down the left side fo the table.

5 Select VLOOKUP from the Lookup and Ref set

6 Click Insert

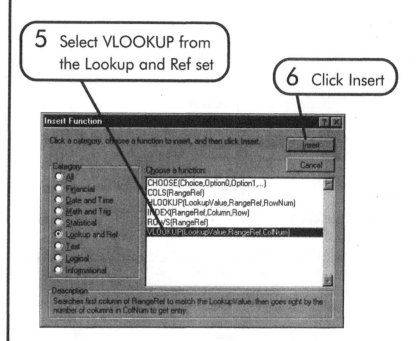

=VLOOKUP(E4,RangeRef,ColNum)

After the first dummy, you will have to highlight the dummies yourself before you can replace them with a pulled-in reference.

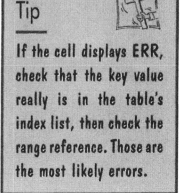

Tip

If the cell displays ERR, check that the key value really is in the table's index list, then check the range reference. Those are the most likely errors.

Customizing the toolbar

In the spreadsheet – and the database – you can change the contents of the toolbar, adding new icons or removing those that you rarely use. It's easy to do – and there is a very handy Reset button which will restore the original button set if you make a mess of it!

The extra buttons are grouped according to the menu position of the matching command.

Basic steps

1 From the Tools menu select Customize Toolbar...

2 Select a Category.

3 Click on a button to read its Description.

4 To add a button, drag and drop it onto the toolbar where you want it to go.

5 To remove a button, drag it off the toolbar.

6 Click ▭OK▭.

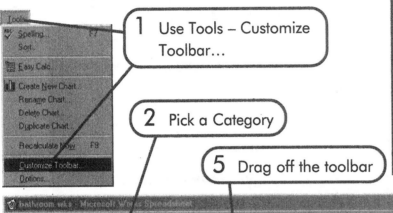

1 Use Tools – Customize Toolbar...

2 Pick a Category

5 Drag off the toolbar

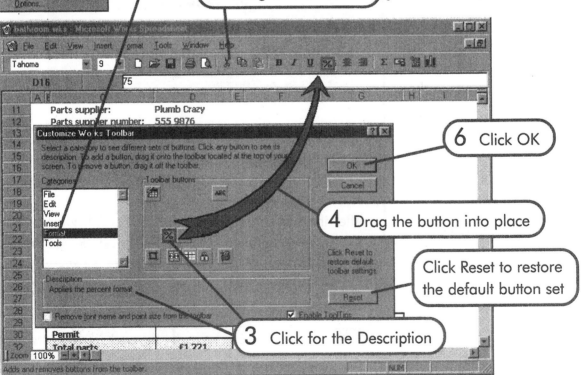

6 Click OK

4 Drag the button into place

Click Reset to restore the default button set

3 Click for the Description

Basic steps

1 From the Tools menu select Options...

2 On the General tab, set the Units of measurement and the Dictionary.

3 On the View tab, turn the Visual Clues on or off as required.

4 On the Data Entry tab, set the data entry mode and Cell Values display/recalculation options.

5 Click ▓ OK ▓.

Other options

The spreadsheet has a limited number of options that you can set to control the screen display and the way it works.

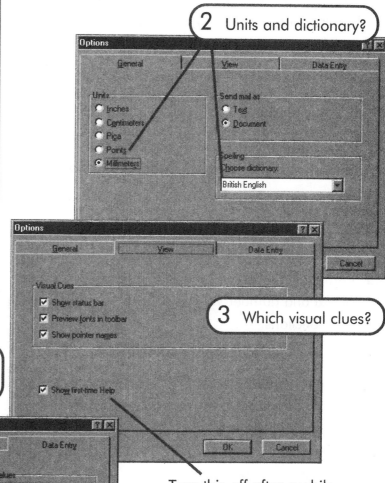

2 Units and dictionary?

3 Which visual clues?

4 Set the mode and value-handling options

5 Click OK

Turn this off after a while

This is normally off so that the sheet recalculates whenever data is edited – there are a few special cases where you need to be able to control when formulae are recalculated

Summary

❑ A spreadsheet is a grid of cells, each identified by its row and column reference. A cell's contents and its display may differ. Formulae are shown by their resulting values; text may be cropped short and numbers shown as hashes in narrow columns.

❑ Rows and columns can be selected by their header numbers and letters; blocks are selected by dragging one corner to the opposite one.

❑ The appearance of a sheet can be enhanced by the use of fonts, alignments, borders and shading.

❑ Numbers can be displayed in different formats.

❑ The Autoformat options provide a quick way to give a professional finish to tables.

❑ Formulae all start with = and may include a mixture of text and number values, cell and range reference and functions.

❑ You can use names to identify cells and ranges.

❑ There is a wide range of functions, organised into several categories. They are easily accessed through the Insert Function dialog box.

❑ The Lookup functions allow you to write formulae that will extract information from a table.

❑ You can add extra buttons to the toolbar, and remove those that you do not use.

6 Working with tables

Copying and filling

The usual **Edit Copy**, **Cut** and **Paste** facilities are available here, as anywhere else in Windows, but there are also alternatives which may be better. Much of your copying is likely to be of formulae to create a table. For this, the **Fill Right** and **Fill Down** commands are quicker and simpler. They will take the formula in the first cell of a range and copy it into all the other cells, adjusting the references as they go, so that the formulae continue to apply to the same relative cells.

For example, if you had a formula in C2 that read:

= A2 * B2

When this is copied down into C3, the formula will read:

= A3 * B3

As you would normally want the same type of formula all down the table, this automatic adjustment of references is generally a good thing.

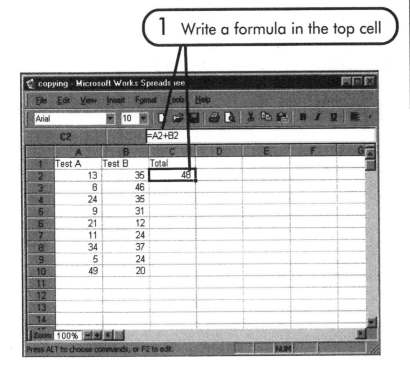

1 Write a formula in the top cell

❑ To Fill Down

1 Write a formula in the cell at the top of the table.

2 Select the range, starting with your formula cell and continuing to the bottom of the table.

3 Open the Edit menu and select Fill Down... or click  if you have added it to the toolbar.

4 Check any of the new formulae and you should see that their references have been adjusted to suit their new positions.

Tip

Fill Right will copy a formula across the base of a table. Add its button to the toolbar for quicker copying.

Fixed references

You may want to copy a formula, but keep a references unchanged. For example, you might want to calculate the VAT on each item in a table, and the VAT rate is stored in one cell.

To keep a reference unchanged, edit the formula and type a $ sign before the column letter and row number.

If C1 held this:

$$= A1 * \$B\$1$$

when copied into C2 it would read:

$$= A2 * \$B\$1$$

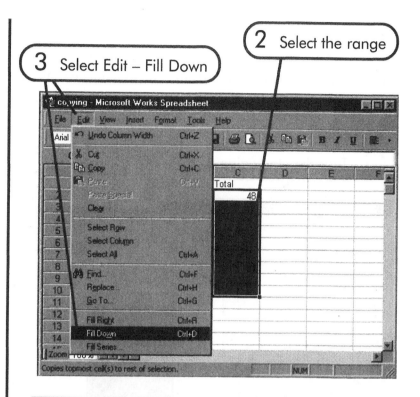

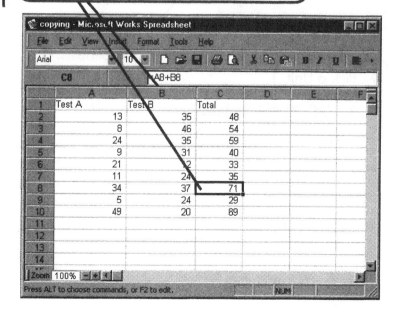

Fill Series

The third option of this type, **Fill Series**, does not copy, but it does create a sequence of numbers or dates. When you are setting up a schedule of work, or any kind of numbered list, it can save a great deal of tedious typing. All the command needs is a starting number or date, and a place to put the series.

1. Type into the top or leftmost cell the first number or date.

2. Select the range which the series will occupy.

3. Open the Edit menu and select Fill Series... or click on ▣ if you have added it to your toolbar.

4. At the dialog box, you will be offered a selection of intervals if you are working with dates. Click the Unit that you want.

5. Type in the Step by value.

6. Click ▭ OK ▭.

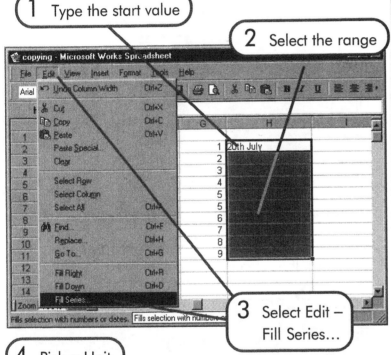

① Type the start value

② Select the range

③ Select Edit – Fill Series...

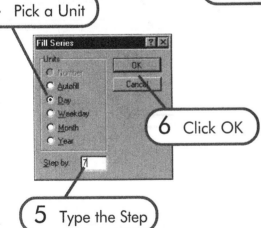

④ Pick a Unit

⑥ Click OK

⑤ Type the Step

Take note

Works recognises dates in several styles. 12/08/00, 12 August 00, 12 aug — though not August 12 (US-style)— will all be taken to mean 12th August 2000. The display can be changed through the Format dialog box.

Basic steps

1 Select the cell(s) to be copied.

2 Open the Edit menu and select Copy, or click on ▣.

3 Select the range into which the data or formulae are to be duplicated.

4 Open the Edit menu and select Paste, or click on ▣.

If you want to copy formulae or data anywhere other than down or right, you must turn to the **Edit – Copy** and **Paste** commands.

For straightforward one-to-one copying, their use is exactly the same as elsewhere in Windows, but you are not limited to this. You can also do one-to-many copying – duplicating a formula throughout a range.

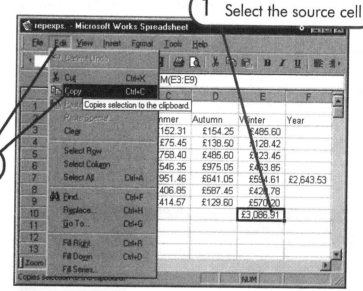

1 Select the source cell

2 Use Edit – Copy

3 Select the target range

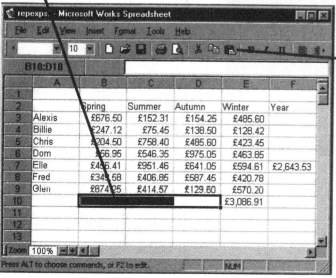

4 Use Edit – Paste

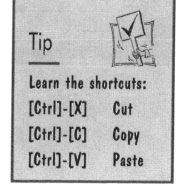

Tip

Learn the shortcuts:

[Ctrl]-[X]   Cut

[Ctrl]-[C]   Copy

[Ctrl]-[V]   Paste

Heights and widths

The spreadsheet grid is not fixed. You can adjust the layout and the column widths and row heights. You can make them bigger to give more room for the contents of cells or to create more space between items, or smaller, to fit more on a page. You can even **hide** rows or columns by adjusting their heights and widths down to zero.

Height and width adjustments are essentially cosmetic. They may improve the presentation of the spreadsheet and make it easier to read, but they will not affect any of the underlying structure or calculations in any way.

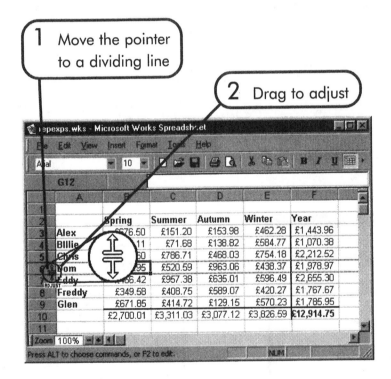

1 Move the pointer to a dividing line

2 Drag to adjust

❑ To adjust a single row

1 Move the pointer to the dividing line below the row you want to adjust.

2 When the pointer changes to the ADJUST double arrow, hold down the mouse button and drag to the desired height.

❑ To adjust a single column

3 Move the pointer to the dividing line to the right of the column you want to adjust.

4 Drag the ADJUST pointer to the desired width.

Take note

Works will automatically adjust the height when you change the font size of any cell in the row.

84

Basic steps

□ **To adjust a set of columns**

1 Select the columns by their letters, or select any block of cells that spans the set.

2 Open the Format menu or right-click for the short menu and select Column Width...

3 Type in a new value in the dialog box. The range is from 0, which will hide them all, and 79 characters, at which one column will fill the screen.

4 Click [OK].

□ **To adjust a set of rows**

5 Follow the steps above, but using the Row Height... command. Heights are given in point sizes. The default is 12 to fit 10 point text.

Multiple adjustments

Dragging the adjust pointer will only change the size of one row or column at a time. If you want to adjust the size of a set of them in one fell swoop, you must tackle it through the **Column Width** dialog box.

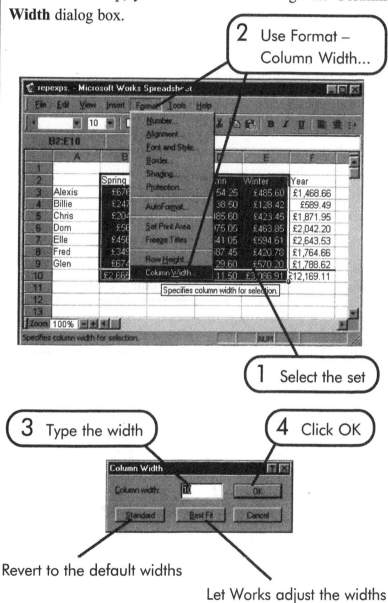

2 Use Format – Column Width...

1 Select the set

3 Type the width

4 Click OK

Revert to the default widths

Let Works adjust the widths to suit the contents

Hidden rows and columns

You may have a spreadsheet which contains confidential material, but which you want to be able to use openly. An invoicing sheet, for example, might have formulae and percentages to calculate your overheads. You want to print customers' copies from this sheet, but without revealing your secrets. The problem can be solved by hiding the rows or columns that contain the sensitive data. Of course, if you drag a height or width to zero by accident, the hiding becomes the problem!

To recover hidden rows and columns, you must first select them. You cannot do this with the mouse as you cannot see them. The only way is to use the **Go To** facility to leap to a cell in the hidden area. The height or width can then be restored via the **Format** menu.

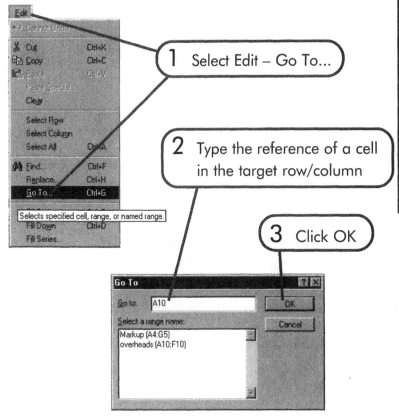

1 Select Edit – Go To...

2 Type the reference of a cell in the target row/column

3 Click OK

☐ To hide rows or columns

Drag the dividing line up or left until it meets the line on the opposite side of the row or column.

☐ To restore hidden rows or columns

1 Open the Edit menu and select Go To...

2 Type in the reference of any cell in the row.

3 Click [OK].

4 By going to the cell, you have selected it, and its row or column. You can now use the Format menu to adjust the height or width (see previous page).

Tip

If you have given your hidden range a Name, you can pick it from the list when you want to Go To it.

Basic steps

❑ To move a row

1 Click on the number to select the row.

2 Move the pointer into the grid area, near the bottom of the row.

3 When the pointer changes from the cross to the DRAG arrow, hold down the mouse button and move the row to its new place.

4 Release the button and the row will insert itself between the existing rows.

❑ To move a column

Follow the same steps as above, but look for the DRAG arrow by the right of the column.

The spreadsheet layout is not fixed. At any point you can move, insert or delete rows or columns, or move blocks of cells.

1 Select the whole row

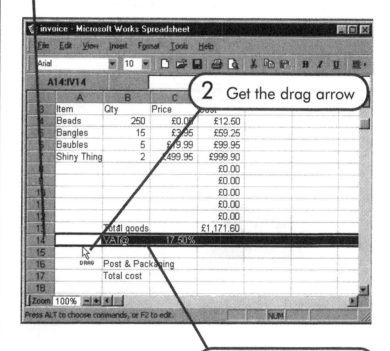

2 Get the drag arrow

3 Pull to its new place

Take note

When you move any cells containing formulae, you may have to change their cell references for the formulae to continue to have the same effect.

Moving blocks

Moving blocks of cells is different from moving rows or columns. The process is the same, and cell references in formulae are adjusted in the same way, but the effects on the sheet are different.

When you move a full row or column into a new position, existing lines make space for it, and the hole that it left is closed up. When you move a block, you lift its data and formulae out of the cells and place them in the new location. A hole is left behind, and the moved contents will overwrite anything that was there before.

Basic steps

❑ To move a block

1 Select the block.

2 Place the cross pointer over any of the edges or corners to get the DRAG arrow.

3 Drag the outline to its new position, taking care not to overlap any wanted data.

4 Release to drop the block into its new position.

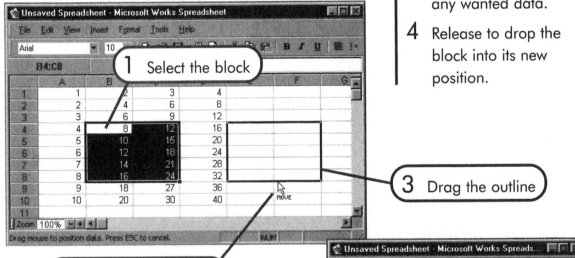

1 Select the block

2 Get the drag arrow

3 Drag the outline

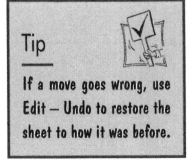

Tip

If a move goes wrong, use Edit — Undo to restore the sheet to how it was before.

The moved block will overwrite existing data

Basic steps

Inserting and deleting

□ To insert rows or columns

1 Select as many rows/ columns as you want to insert, at the place where you want them to go.

2 Right click for the short menu or open the Insert menu and select Row/Column. Existing rows will move down, columns move right to make room.

□ To delete rows or columns

3 Select the rows/col- umns you want to delete.

4 Open short menu or the Insert menu and select Delete Row/ Column.

You can only insert or delete rows or columns, and not blocks within the sheet. Bear in mind that it is the *whole* row, or column, that is removed. If the occupied area of your sheet extends beyond the visible screen, check along the line to see if there is any data elsewhere that you would prefer not to lose.

There are optional buttons to cover all four insert/delete row/ column combinations. If you have to do a major restructure of a sheet, add them to the toolbar.

 Insert row   **Delete row**

Insert column   **Delete column**

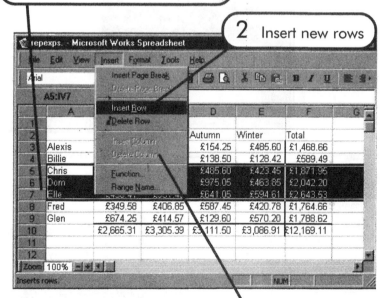

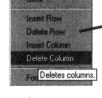

If a single cell or a block is selected when you open the menu, both Row and Column Insert and Delete commands are available.

Delete commands are also on the Insert menu

89

Sorting

Where you have a table of data organised, database-wise, so that each row holds details of one contact, customer, stock item or whatever, this can be sorted into order. The sort can be ascending or descending, numeric or alphabetic, and can be based on up to three columns. A contact list, for example, could be sorted first by County, then by Town and finally by Name.

1 Select the block to be sorted.

2 Open the Tools menu and select Sort...

3 At the first dialog box, chose Sort all the information if all of the data in the sheet is part of the database. If there are other things as well, select Sort only the high-lighted information.

4 Pick the column on which to sort.

5 Choose the order – Ascending or De-scending.

6 To sort on more than one column, click Advanced.

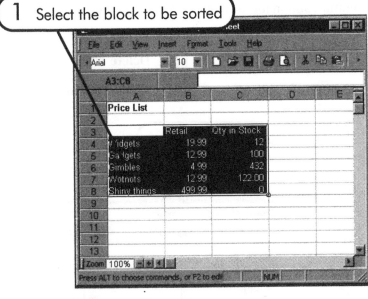

1 Select the block to be sorted

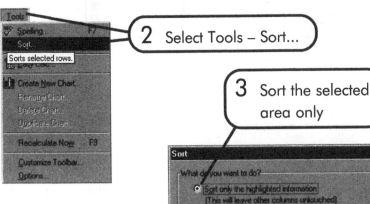

2 Select Tools – Sort...

3 Sort the selected area only

7 Repeat steps 5 and 6.

8 If the selected block includes headings, set the Header rows option.

9 Click [Sort].

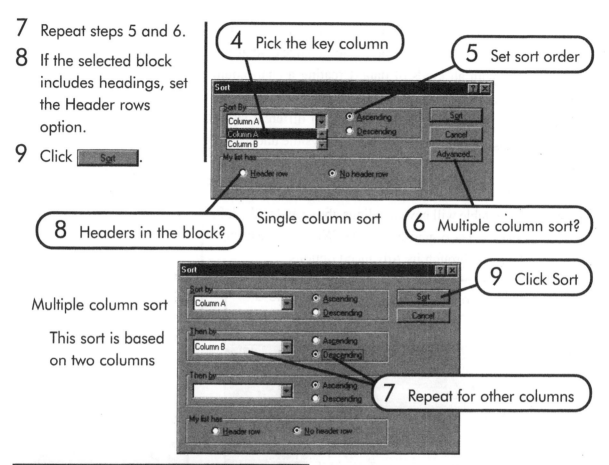

4 Pick the key column

5 Set sort order

8 Headers in the block?

Single column sort

6 Multiple column sort?

Multiple column sort

This sort is based on two columns

9 Click Sort

7 Repeat for other columns

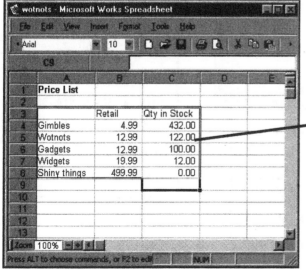

The rows have been first sorted into *Ascending* order of Price, then on *Descending* order of number in Stock.

Charts from tables

Graphs and charts can bring out the underlying patterns in sets of numbers, and with Works you have a good range of charting styles, to cope with all kinds of data. Creating a chart could scarcely be simpler, and once created, a chart can easily be adapted. A few minutes' experimenting with different styles should be enough to find one that best displays the underlying patterns.

To create a chart, you must first have a table of figures. Works assumes that the table will have headings above and to the left, and that the data will be organised in rows. Works can also cope with other layouts, through its Advanced options.

1 Select the block of cells containing the figures and their headings.

2 Open the Tools menu and select Create New Chart... or click [icon] on the toolbar.

3 Pick the Type. (N.B. It can be changed later.)

4 Add a Title, Border and Gridlines if wanted.

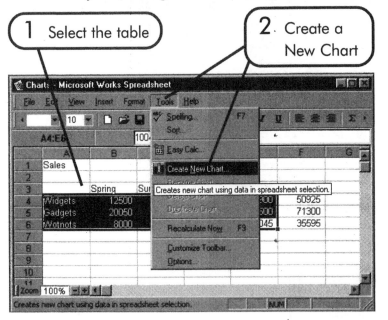

1 Select the table

2. Create a New Chart

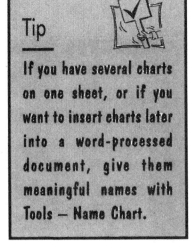

Tip

If you have several charts on one sheet, or if you want to insert charts later into a word-processed document, give them meaningful names with Tools — Name Chart.

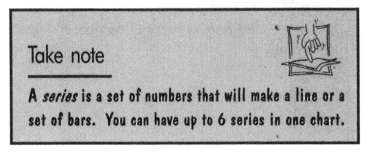

Take note

A *series* is a set of numbers that will make a line or a set of bars. You can have up to 6 series in one chart.

☐ If your table is non-standard...

5 Open the Advanced Options tab.

6 If your series run down the columns, click on the Down option.

7 If the First column does not contain headings, click on Category.

8 If the First row does not contain headings, click on Y values.

9 Click [OK].

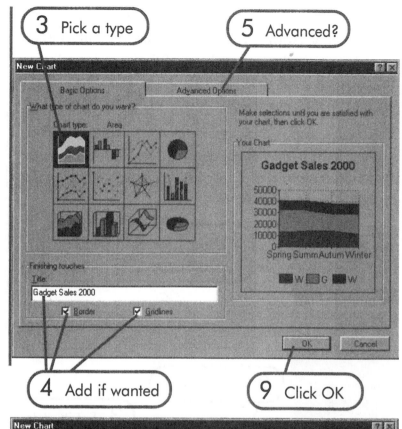

3 Pick a type

5 Advanced?

4 Add if wanted

9 Click OK

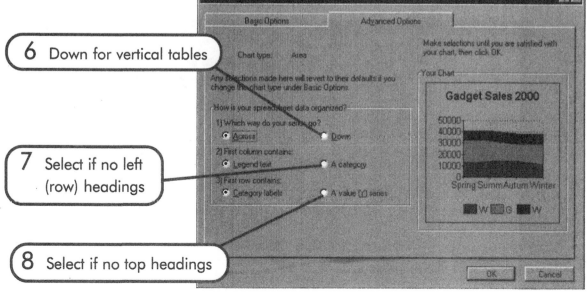

6 Down for vertical tables

7 Select if no left (row) headings

8 Select if no top headings

Tailor-made charts

A chart appears in a window of its own, not within the spreadsheet, and when that window is on top, you will see a new set of buttons in the toolbar. Most of these are for selecting different chart types, and there is another new one that will take you back to the spreadsheet at the site of the first series.

If you want to make significant changes to the chart, you are best working through the Format menu options. To alter the font, style or other property of an individual item, right-click on it for its short menu in the usual way.

❑ To change patterns

1 Open the Format menu and select Shading and Color...

2 Click the Series you want to reformat.

3 Select a fill or line Color and a Pattern.

4 Click **Format** to fix your choices.

5 Repeat steps 2 to 4 for each series.

6 Close the dialog box.

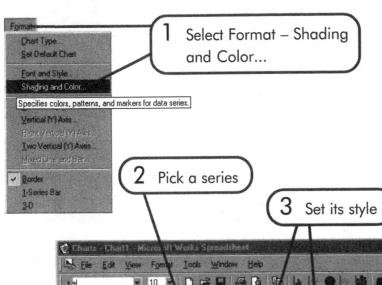

1 Select Format – Shading and Color...

2 Pick a series

3 Set its style

Go to first series on spreadsheet

4 Fix the format

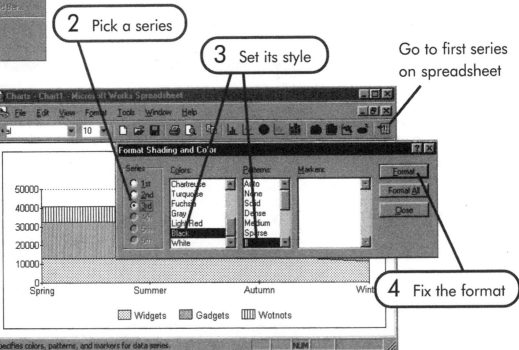

❑ To change the type

1 Open the Format menu, select Chart Type and pick a Basic Type.

or

2 Click on a type button on the Chart toolbar.

3 Open the Variations tab.

4 Select the type, checking its appearance in the preview panel.

5 Click ▢ OK ▢.

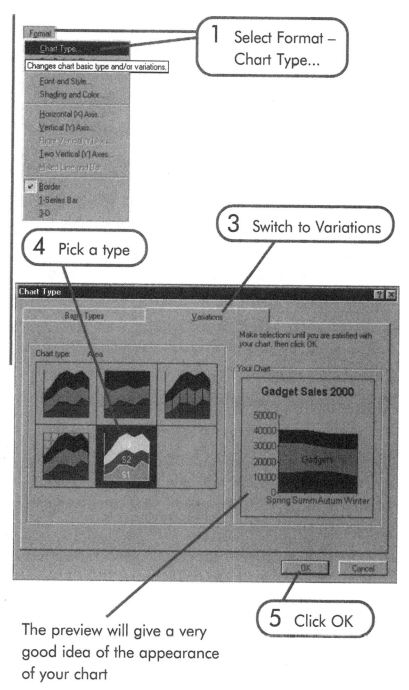

1 Select Format – Chart Type...

3 Switch to Variations

4 Pick a type

5 Click OK

The preview will give a very good idea of the appearance of your chart

95

Summary

❑ Data and formulae can be copied either with Copy and Paste or with Fill Right and Fill Down.

❑ Use Fill Series to create a set of numbers or dates.

❑ When formulae are copied, cell and range references are normally adjusted to suit the new positions. References can be made absolute, so that they are not changed when the formula is copied.

❑ You can adjust the height of rows and the width of columns. If reduced to zero, the lines are hidden.

❑ Hidden rows and columns can be restored by using Go To, to move to a cell in the hidden area, and then increasing the height or width.

❑ If rows, columns are moved, existing rows and columns will shuffle up to make room for them. If blocks are moved, they overwrite any existing data.

❑ Rows and columns can be inserted or deleted.

❑ Data can be sorted on the values held in selected columns.

❑ There are a wide variety of chart types, designed to meet a range of display needs. They can be selected from the toolbar buttons.

❑ Charts can be given meaningful Names to make them easier to find later.

❑ When a chart window is active, the Format menu has a new set of commands.

❑ Colours and shading that work well on screen, may not work as well when printed. Check your choices by switching to Display as Printed view.

7 Working with data

What is a database?

A database is a collection of *records*, each of which will contain data about one person, company, stock item or whatever. The record is split into *fields*, each of which will hold the same kind of data in every record.

The database can be viewed as a *List*, where it will look like a table in a spreadsheet, with each record occupying its own row, and the fields running down the columns. It can also be viewed as a set of *Forms*, where the data for each record is laid out as it might be in a card-index system.

By applying *filters*, you can pull out groups of records that have specified values in particular fields. You could find, for example, all your customers who lived in Macclesfield, or those stock items which need to be reordered.

The reports that can be produced from a database may include all its records, or just a set that has been selected by a filter. They may show all the available data for each record, or only that from selected fields. In this way, the same database can produce mailing labels to send a circular to all your customers, and a list of those who owe money, showing the amounts and the age of each debt.

Data can be copied to and from a spreadsheet, so that you can perform there the calculations that cannot be done in the database. Names, addresses and other data from a database can be combined with standard letters to produced mailshots (see *Mail merge*, page 130).

Tip

There are a number of TaskWizards that will create databases. If you want an address book, accounts or inventory system, check out the TaskWizards before you start to create one from scratch.

Preparing the data

The most important stage in creating a database takes place off-screen. You must have your data organised thoroughly first, before you start to think about form and report designs.

The key questions are:

● What do you want to store?

● What do you want to be able to get out of it?

Data must be broken down into the smallest units that you might want to sort on or search for. If you are storing people's names, for instance, you would normally break them into three fields, Title, Initials (or Forenames) and Surname. The records could then be sorted alphabetically (by Surname), and you could search for someone by their Forename or Surname. It is crucial to get this right from the very start, as you cannot split data up, once it has been typed in.

Works stores database data in the same way that it stores spreadsheet data, and it can display it using the same range of formats. The main ones are:

● Text

● Number

● Date

When you create the database, set a format for each field that will suit its data. Put dates in a text field, and you cannot do much with them. Put them in a Date field, and you can sort records into date order, or search for those before or after a given date.

Creating a database

Plan the structure of your database, and write down the names and formats of the fields it will have. Take a sample of your data and check that it will fit into your structure. Does it work? Yes? Then it time to put it into Works.

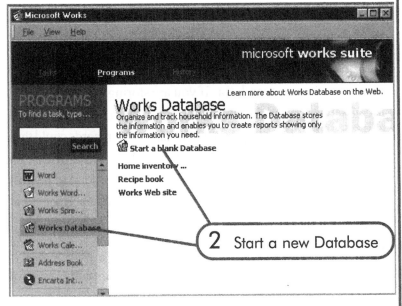

2 Start a new Database

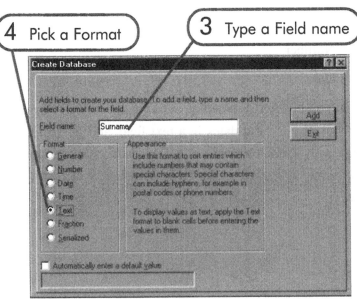

4 Pick a Format

3 Type a Field name

Basic steps

1 Start up Works, or open the File menu and select New.

2 Go to Works Tools and click on Database.

3 Type the Field name for your first field.

4 Set a suitable Format.

5 With *Date, Time* and *Number* formats, select an Appearance.

6 Click [Add].

7 Repeat for all fields.

8 Click [Done].

9 Save the database – and save it regularly while you work to keep your data safe.

Take note

Mistakes are not permanent! You can change a field's format in List or Form Design view. Field names can also be changed later.

Tip

If you want to give ID numbers to your records, include a Serialized field. This will automatically number each new record as you create it.

5 Set the Appearance

6 Click Add

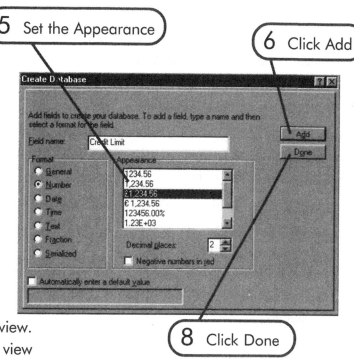

The new database opens in List view. You may want to switch to Form view for easier data entry. (See page 103.)

8 Click Done

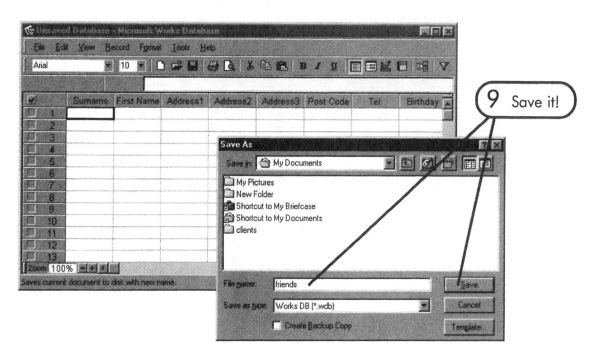

9 Save it!

List and Form views

In List view you can see a screenful of records at a time, though not all of the fields will necessarily be in sight. It is useful when you want to check, or edit, the values in the same fields of different records, and it is simpler to hunt through the database when you can see 15 or 20 records at a time.

The view looks like a spreadsheet, and is handled in much the same way. Things are not exactly the same – the main differences are given on the right.

You can adjust the heights of records and the widths of fields, and note that the changes you make here are not carried over into the Form view. You can also move, insert and delete records and fields. All of these operations are carried out as with the rows and columns of the spreadsheet (see *Adjusting the layout*, page 87).

There are no Format options on the short menu in List view. Use the Format menu if you want to reformat fields.

- ❑ Fonts, borders and shading cannot be applied to a single cell or block. They always apply to whole fields.

- ❑ When sorting, do not select a block. The sort always works on the whole database.

- ❑ Insert Record ⬛ Delete Record ⬛ and Insert Field ⬛ have buttons. There is no button for Delete Field – this mustn't be too easy! Use Record – Delete Field, or delete it in Form Design view.

Click to go to Form view

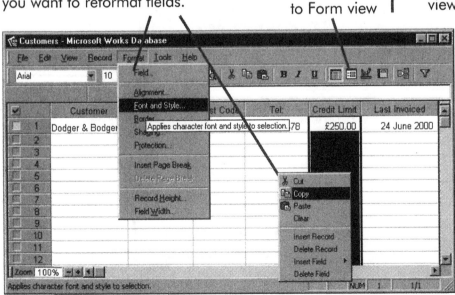

Applies character font and style to selection.

Basic steps

❏ To edit a field

1 Move to the record.

2 Move to the field.

3 Either press [F2] or click the insertion point into the text in the entry line.

4 When you have done, click ☑ or press [Enter] to accept the changes, click ☒ or press [Escape] to leave it unchanged.

❏ To move with keys

[Tab] – next field

[Shift]+[Tab] – previous field

[Ctrl]+[PageDown] – next record

[Ctrl]+[PageUp] – previous record

[Ctrl]+[Home] – first record

[Ctrl]+[End] – last record

Using Form view

The Form view is generally the best one to use when entering data or updating records. You would normally be working on one record at a time, and all its details will be to hand. You can easily move between fields and between adjacent records, either with the mouse or the keyboard.

When you want to get a wider view of the database, or make comparisons between records, switch to List view by clicking ▦ on the toolbar.

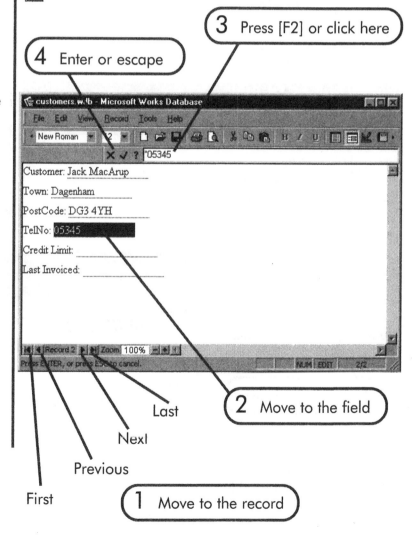

3 Press [F2] or click here

4 Enter or escape

2 Move to the field

Last

Next

Previous

First

1 Move to the record

Designing the form

When you start a new database, the system sets up a simple form. At any point you can go into Form Design view to change the layout, add *labels* (headings, notes or other text), *graphics* – even new *fields*, if required.

Design the form with screen use in mind. You can print it, but most of your database printing will be as reports, or mailing labels and mailmerge letters via the word processor.

Selecting fields and other items

As elsewhere in Works, you must select items before you can change their format, move and resize them.

❑ To select a set of adjacent objects

1 Imagine a rectangle that will enclose the items and click at one of its corners.

2 Drag to draw an outline around them.

❑ To select a set of scattered items

3 Click on the first item.

4 Hold [Ctrl] and click on the rest. If you pick one by mistake, click again to deselect it.

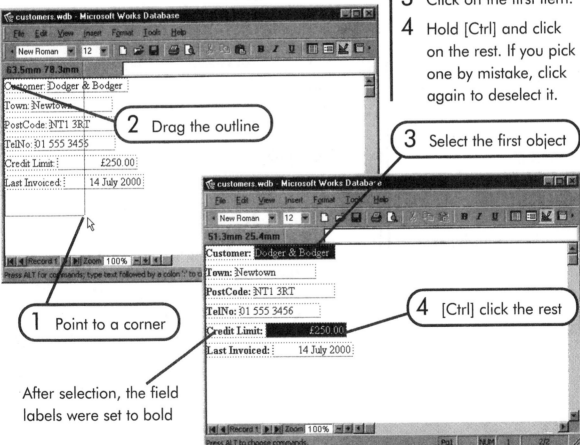

2 Drag the outline

3 Select the first object

1 Point to a corner

4 [Ctrl] click the rest

After selection, the field labels were set to bold

104

Basic steps

❑ To move items

1 Select the item(s).

2 Move the pointer over them until the DRAG prompt shows.

3 Hold down the mouse button and move to the new location.

4 Release the button to drop into place.

❑ To resize an item

5 Select it.

6 Point to an edge to get the RESIZE arrow.

7 Drag the outline to required size.

8 Release the button.

Items can be moved at any time, even after you have started to enter data. Fields can also be resized if you find that data items are larger – or smaller – than anticipated. Changing the width only changes how much is displayed. It has no effect on the data in the fields.

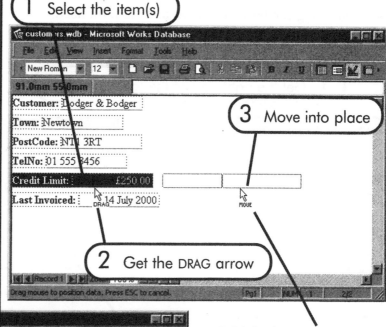

1 Select the item(s)

3 Move into place

2 Get the DRAG arrow

DRAG changes to MOVE when you move the item

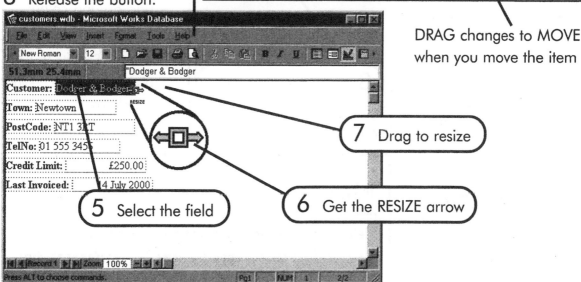

7 Drag to resize

5 Select the field

6 Get the RESIZE arrow

Presentation

The form can be enhanced in a number of ways:

- **Fonts** and **Alignments** are set here the same as elsewhere – select the items and adjust the settings.

- **Rectangles** can be added to give a background or decorative border around a set of fields.

- **Shading** can be set for fields and the form itself.

- **Borders** can be applied to fields or labels.

❑ To add a rectangle

1 Adjust the position of the form in the window so that you can see the place where the rectangle is to go.

2 Open the Insert menu and select Rectangle.

3 A shadow rectangle will be dropped into the top left corner. Drag it and resize it as required.

4 Right-click on the rectangle for its short menu and select Borders or Shading. Set its line style and background colour.

5 Open the Format menu and use Send to Back to put the rectangle behind your fields.

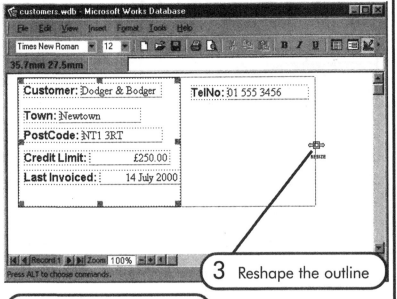

1 Get the right part of the form into view

3 Reshape the outline

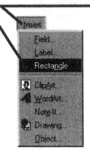

2 Select Insert – Rectangle

Take note

Fields' names and data areas are separate items. Select them together if you want to apply the same font, border or shading.

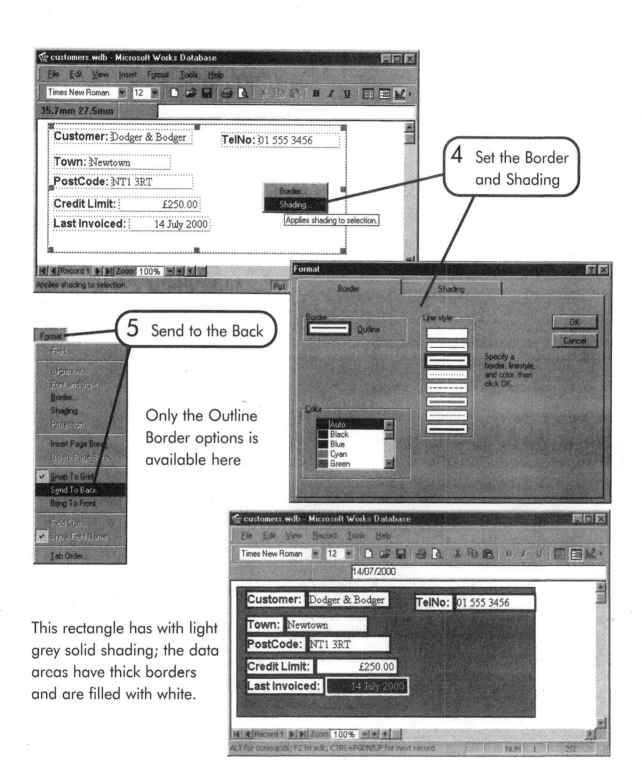

4 Set the Border and Shading

5 Send to the Back

Only the Outline Border options is available here

This rectangle has with light grey solid shading; the data areas have thick borders and are filled with white.

Searching for records

If you want to find a record, or pick out a set of records that share some common values, then you must create a Filter. In this you define what value, or range of values, you are looking for in a particular field. At the simplest you might look for the person with the surname 'Jones', or pick out all those customers whose debts were over their credit limits.

For the first of these, you would search the *Customer* field, using the comparison 'is equal to' with the value 'Jones'.

For the second example, you would search the *Amount Owing* field, using the comparison 'is greater than' and comparing it to the *Credit Limit* field.

If you want to get more complicated, you might set up a filter to find, for example, those clients in Manchester that do not owe money and haven't received a vist from the rep in the last month.

Filters are saved with the database and can be recalled and reused later, so even if it takes you a little while to set up a filter to pick out exactly the right set of records, at least you only have to do it once.

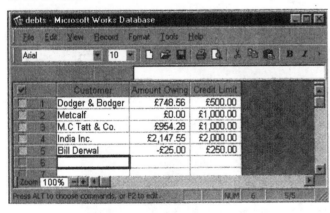

The examples shown here are based on this set of records

1 Open the Tools menu and select Filters... or click [🖫] to open the Filters dialog box.

2 Click [New Filter] – you won't need to for your very first filter.

3 Give the filter a name to remind you what sort of records it finds.

4 From the Field name list, pick the field that contains the values you are looking for.

5 Pull down the Comparison list and pick a comparison.

6 Type a value or a field name into the Compare To slot.

7 Click [Apply Filter].

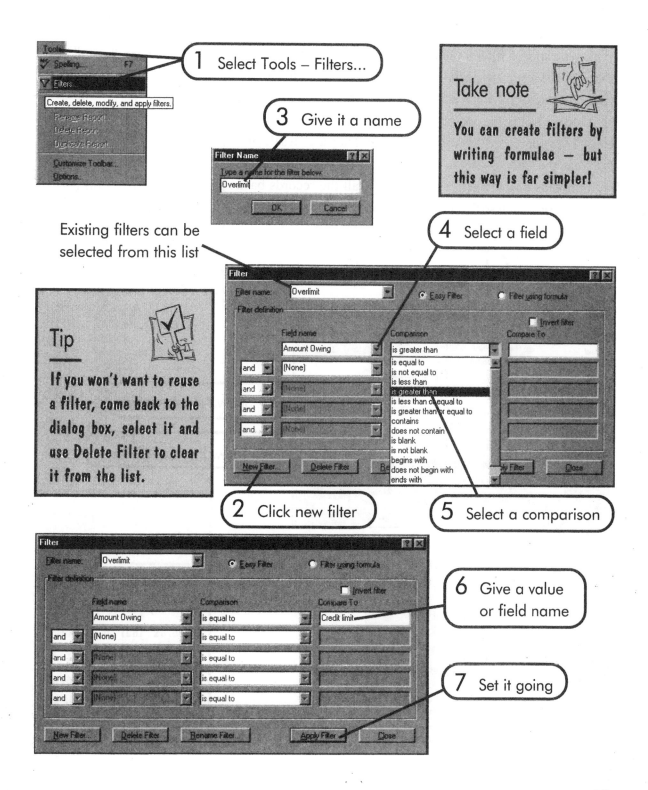

1 Select Tools – Filters...

3 Give it a name

Take note

You can create filters by writing formulae — but this way is far simpler!

Existing filters can be selected from this list

4 Select a field

Tip

If you won't want to reuse a filter, come back to the dialog box, select it and use Delete Filter to clear it from the list.

2 Click new filter

5 Select a comparison

6 Give a value or field name

7 Set it going

109

Working with filters

When you apply a filter for the very first time, you may be taken aback by the result – especially if you have been working in List view. Instead of having a screen full of records, you may well be faced with only the odd one or two! Where have all the other 10,000 of your records gone? Don't panic. They are all safe, it's just that the only ones on display are those that match the requirements of the filter. You can bring all the records back into view, or switch so that those that didn't match are displayed – and the matching ones are hidden.

Basic steps

- ❑ To restore the full set
- 1 Open the Record menu.
- 2 Select Show then All Records.
- ❑ To switch found and hidden records
- 3 Open the Record menu.
- 4 Select Show then Hidden Records.

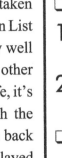
1 Open the Record menu

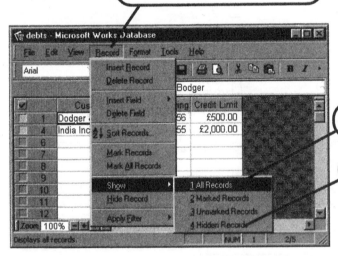

2 Show All the records

4 Show the hidden ones

Tip

When you want to reuse a filter, select it from the Record – Apply Filter menu.

Take note

After a Filter has been applied, you only see the records that match the search requirements. If you produce a report now, only these records will be included in the output.

Basic steps

❑ To mark a record

1 Click in the box to its left.

❑ To mark a set

2 Apply a filter to select the set, then click the top left checkbox.

❑ To display marked records

3 Open the Record menu, select Show then Marked Records.

Marking records

Simple filters are good for finding sets of records that match one criterion. If you want to find records that match two or more alternative criteria, there are two approaches.

● Create multi-line filters, linking the lines by OR. For example, the search might be for 'Town is equal to Leeds' OR 'Town is equal to London'. This can get complicated.

● Create and apply several simple filters, and after each has been run, mark the records that are filtered out. You can then display all marked records, to bring together the results of the separate filters.

2 Mark all displayed records

1 Mark the record

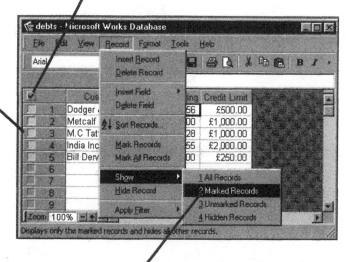

3 Display all marked records

Tip

Sometimes it is easier to filter out the records you do not want — rather than those that you do. If you mark them, then Show the Unmarked Records, you will see the ones you wanted.

Reports

The database's report routines produce lists of the data held in the records. You have a little control over the layout, but full control of the content. You can:

- select the fields to be included in the reports;
- sort and group on one or more fields;
- restrict the report to filtered, or marked, records;
- include a variety of summary statistics.

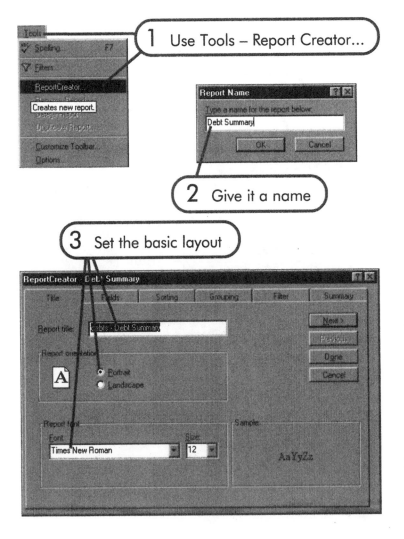

1 Use Tools – Report Creator...

2 Give it a name

3 Set the basic layout

1 Open the Tools menu and select Report Creator ...

2 Type in a name for your report.

❑ Work through the tabs, clicking [Next >] after each.

3 On the Title tab, check and edit the basic layout – title, page orientation and font.

4 On the Fields tab, select the field to be included and click [Add >] after each.

5 For sorted output, on the Sorting tab select a field to Sort by and set *Ascending* or *Descending* order.

6 On the Grouping tab, if you have set a *Sort by* field, you can also opt to group on this field. Use this where records may have the same value in the *Sort by* field, e.g. Town.

cont...

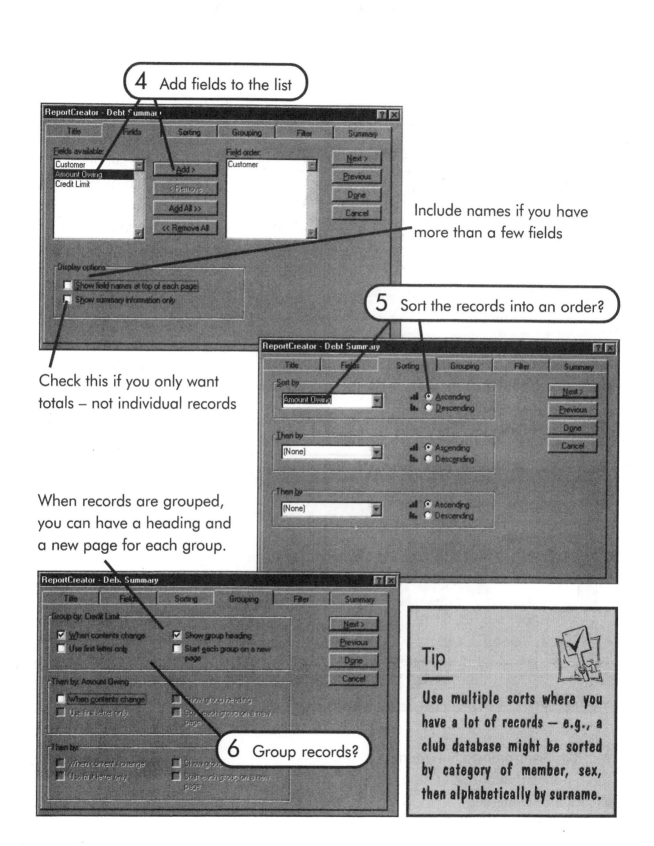

4 Add fields to the list

Include names if you have more than a few fields

Check this if you only want totals – not individual records

5 Sort the records into an order?

When records are grouped, you can have a heading and a new page for each group.

6 Group records?

Tip

Use multiple sorts where you have a lot of records — e.g., a club database might be sorted by category of member, sex, then alphabetically by surname.

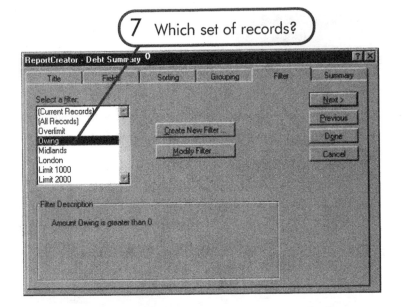

7 Which set of records?

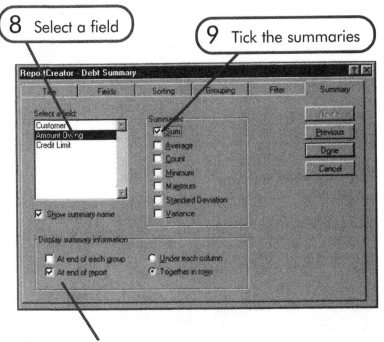

8 Select a field

9 Tick the summaries

With Grouped reports, Summaries can be printed after each group, or all together at the end

...continued

7 On the Filter tab, select the set of records to be output. These can be all records, the current displayed set or those from a filter.

8 On the Summary tab, select a field for which you want one or more summary figures.

9 Tick the Summaries you want for that field.

10 Repeat 8 and 9 for all the fields that are to have summaries.

Take note

If you do not have a suitable filter, you can create one while you are on the Filter tab.

Improved outputs

When the report is complete, you will be offered a preview – use it. If you do not like the appearance, you can adjust it in Report view. Titles and headings can be changed if necessary, using the normal editing methods. You can also adjust column widths, change text and number formats and add borders and shading.

Could be bigger

Needs Currency format

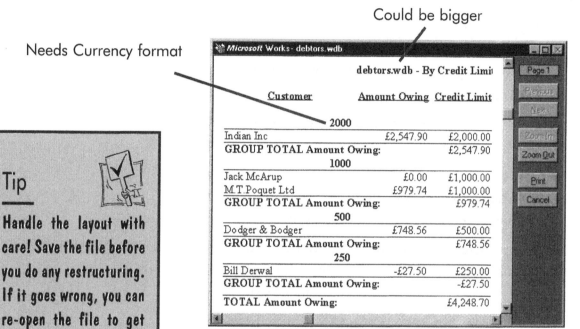

Tip

Handle the layout with care! Save the file before you do any restructuring. If it goes wrong, you can re-open the file to get back to where you were.

Select and format cell contents as you would in the spreadsheet

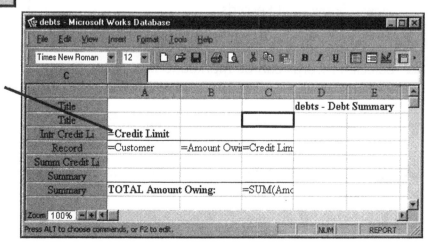

Summary

- A database is a collection of records, with fields holding the separate details for each record.

- If you organise your data before you start to create the database, you will save yourself trouble.

- In List view you can see many records at once; Form view displays only one record – but more clearly – and is preferred for data entry.

- You can adjust the appearance of the form through Form Design view.

- Fields' widths, and their locations can be adjusted at any time without affecting any data they may hold.

- Text can be formatted in the usual way, but borders only apply to individual items. If you want a box around a set of items, insert a rectangle.

- Filters search for those records that have particular values in given fields. The comparison can be with actual values, or the values in another field.

- After a filter has been applied you can only see those records that match. To see the rest again, use View – Show – All Records.

- To reuse a filter, select it from the Apply Filter list.

- Selected records can be marked to keep them together.

- Reports list the chosen fields for a set of records. They can include summary values.

- The appearance of the report can be adjusted by editing it in Report view.

8 Working together

Inserting objects

Draw, Clip Art and WordArt graphics, charts, database fields and other objects from other Windows applications can be inserted into word processor documents and database forms. Whatever the type of object, the techniques are much the same. In these examples, the objects are bitmap pictures from Paint.

When first inserted, an object will push any existing text out of its way and sit by itself on the left of the page, as above. This is its *In Line with text* Wrapping style, and in this you can change its size, drag it to another line and set its left–right alignment. The alternative *Square* and *Tight* Wrapping styles gives you more flexibility. In these it can be embedded within text, and positioned anywhere on the page. In *Tight* style, the text will be fitted close to the outline of the object; in *Square* style, the object will sit in a cleared rectangle.

Basic steps

❑ To insert an object

1 Place the insertion pointer where you want the object to go.

2 Open the Insert menu and select the type of object – Picture (see page 121), Text Box, Spreadsheet (see page 128) or Object.

3 Find or create the object – techniques vary with the type. With an Object, you can create a new one by selecting the type or use an existing file.

2 Open the Insert menu and select the object type

3 Find or create the object

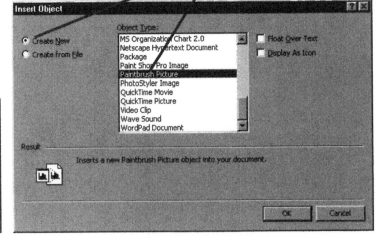

Insert Object

Object Type:

Create New
Create from File

MS Organization Chart 2.0
Netscape Hypertext Document
Package
Paint Shop Pro Image
Paintbrush Picture
PhotoStyler Image
QuickTime Movie
QuickTime Picture
Video Clip
Wave Sound
WordPad Document

☐ Float Over Text
☐ Display As Icon

Result

Inserts a new Paintbrush Picture object into your document.

OK   Cancel

Tip

There are toolbar buttons to insert all the Works objects.

Formatting objects

- ❏ To change Wrap mode
- 1 Select the object.
- 2 From the Format menu select Object...
- 3 Go to the Wrapping tab.
- 4 Pick the Style.
- ❏ To set an exact size
- 5 Switch to the Size tab.
- 6 Set the Height and Width values, and the Rotation, if required.

Objects can be resized or moved with the usual click and drag mouse methods, but can be adjusted more accurately through the Format options.

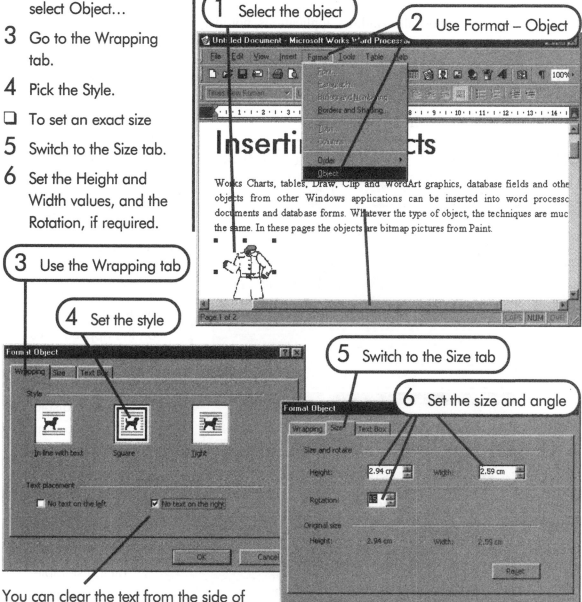

1 Select the object

2 Use Format – Object

3 Use the Wrapping tab

4 Set the style

5 Switch to the Size tab

6 Set the size and angle

You can clear the text from the side of an embedded object if required

Linked objects

A *linked* object is one that was created by another application, and that retains the connection to it within the Works document. Double-clicking on the object activates the link and opens the original application so that the object can be edited.

Linking works with almost all Windows applications, not just the Microsoft add-ons.

When you insert an object, you will be offered the choice of creating a new one or using an existing file. If you create from file, you will be given the option to link.

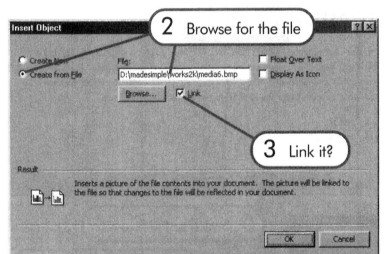

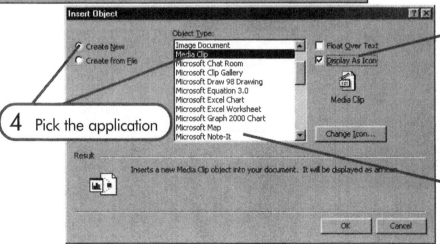

1 Open the Insert menu and select Object...

Either

2 Select Create from file, and browse through your system for the file.

3 Check Link if you want the object to be up- dated when the original file changes.

Or

4 Select Create new, and pick the application.

5 After creating the object, click back into the Works document, or use Update and Exit on the application's File menu.

Use *icon* displays where you want to link to a file, and not make it part of the document

The list will include all the suitable applications on your system

Basic steps

1 Open the Insert menu, point to Picture then select From File...

Or

2 Click 🖼 Insert Picture.

3 Switch to the picture's folder.

4 If there are lots, use the Files of type box to filter out the right type.

5 Pick a picture.

6 Click Open.

Tip

There are many graphics formats, but Works can handle all the common ones, such as **BMP, PIX, JPG, GIF, WMF, TIF.**

'A picture is worth a thousand words.' That philosophy can be applied to many types of documents.

● Your company logo will identify your letter and invoices;

● Products sell better if people can see pictures of them;

● Diagrams are often essential for communicating technical information and other complex concepts.

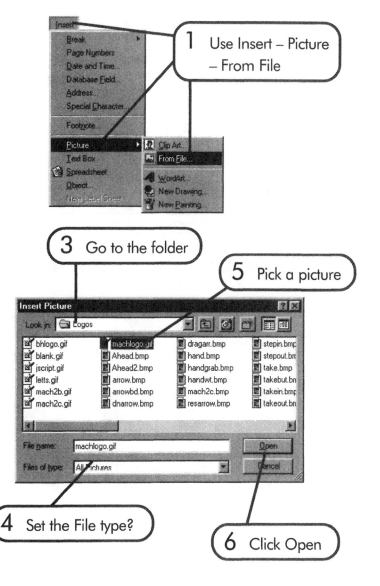

Clip Art

Clip Art pictures from the Clip Gallery can be inserted into any application – but don't overdo it. There's so much Clip Art around that you must use it selectively to have any impact.

Basic steps

1 Use Insert – Picture – Clip Art...

2 At the Pictures panel choose a Category.

Or

3 Type a Search word and press [Enter].

4 Click on a picture.

5 Click  to insert it; to preview it; to add it to your Favorites; to find similar clips.

6 Close the Gallery.

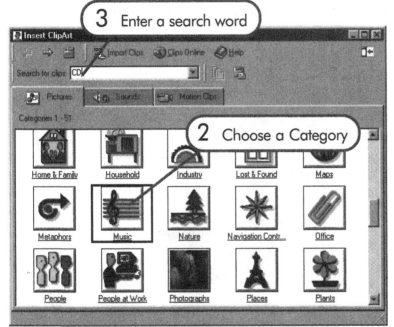

3 Enter a search word

2 Choose a Category

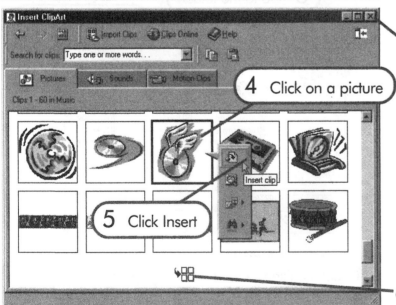

6 Close the Gallery

4 Click on a picture

5 Click Insert

Take note

You cannot insert Sounds into a Works document and the Motion clips only come in as still graphics.

Click here for more pictures

Drawing pictures

1 Open the Insert menu, point to Picture then select New Drawing...

Or

2 Click 🖻 New Drawing.

3 Select an object tool from the Drawing or from the AutoShapes toolbars.

4 Point and drag to create the object.

5 To adjust an object, click on it to select it. It can then be moved, resized, deleted or recoloured.

6 Double-click on an element to open its Format dialog box for fine-tuning its display.

Autoshapes offer a quick way to get neat effects

Basic lines and shapes

Simple diagrams and illustrations can be created within documents using the Drawing facilities. In a Drawing image, each item remains separate and can be moved, resized, recoloured or deleted at any later time. (Though items can be joined into Groups or placed inside picture frames, for convenient handling.) This is quite different from Paint where each addition becomes merged permanently into the whole picture.

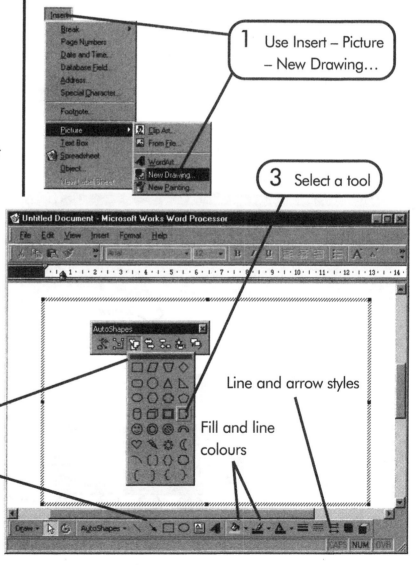

1 Use Insert – Picture – New Drawing...

3 Select a tool

Line and arrow styles

Fill and line colours

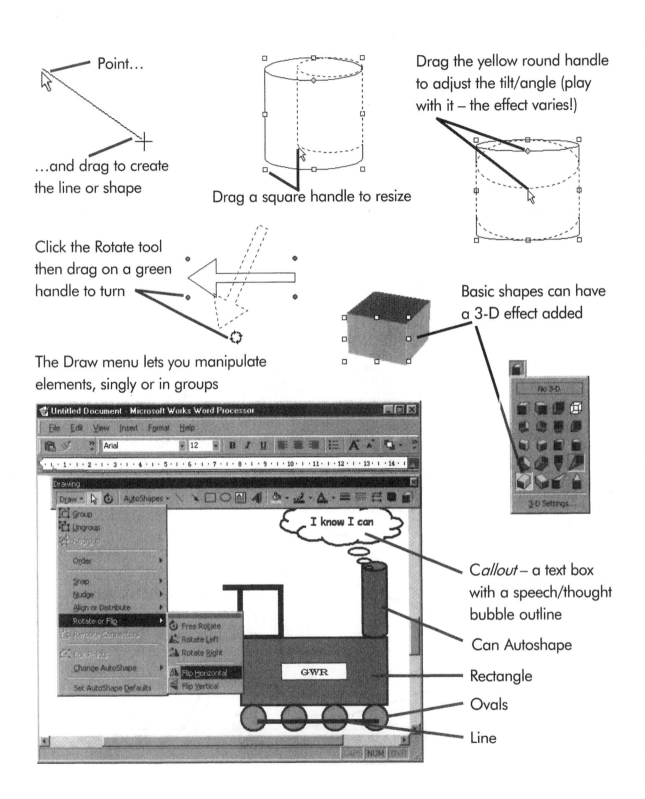

Point...

...and drag to create the line or shape

Drag the yellow round handle to adjust the tilt/angle (play with it – the effect varies!)

Drag a square handle to resize

Click the Rotate tool then drag on a green handle to turn

Basic shapes can have a 3-D effect added

The Draw menu lets you manipulate elements, singly or in groups

Callout – a text box with a speech/thought bubble outline

Can Autoshape

Rectangle

Ovals

Line

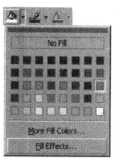

The drop-down palette has a set of basic colours, and access to the full palette (More Fill Colors...) and the Fill Effects dialog box

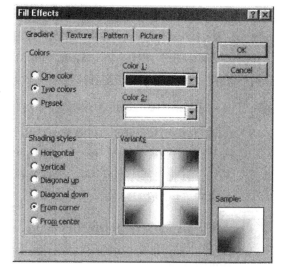

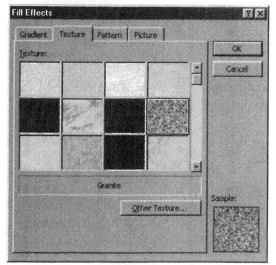

Fill Effects include Gradients and Textures – both good for the backgrounds of boxes. The same Patterns are available here as for Lines.

Double-click to open the Format... dialog box

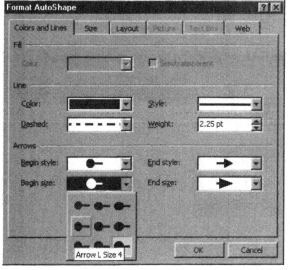

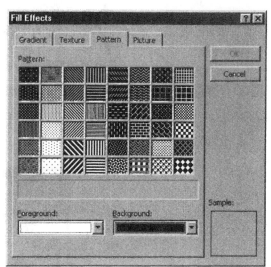

Patterned Lines are reached from the Line Color options. Try them for distinctive frames.

To add arrowheads, select from the Format dialog box.

WordArt

With WordArt, text can be rotated, distorted, shadowed and patterned. The process is fiddly, but it does allow you to make a real splash with text. You could put it to good use it for invitations, adverts, posters, newsletters and the like.

● You cannot resize of the object from within WordArt, and a different effect may require a different sized or shaped area. You may need to switch out of and back into WordArt several times before you get the right balance of shape and size.

● Many shapes will normally occupy only a small area in the middle of the object – click 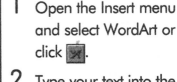 to make the text fill the object area.

Basic steps

1 Open the Insert menu and select WordArt or click 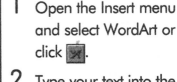.

2 Type your text into the WordArt window.

3 Click [Update Display] to write it to the page.

4 Point and click back into your document.

5 Select the WordArt object and resize it.

6 Double-click on the object to return to WordArt to set the effects. (Expect to do steps 5 and 6 several times before you have finished!)

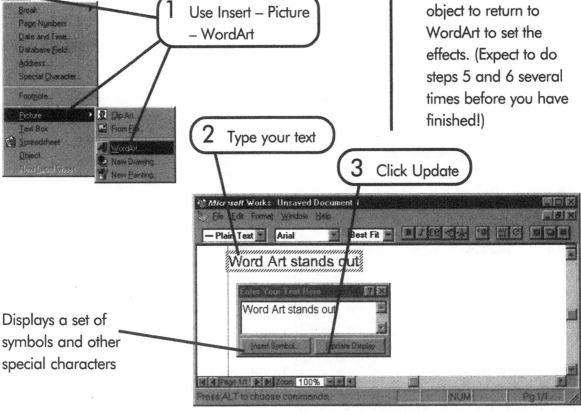

1 Use Insert – Picture – WordArt

2 Type your text

3 Click Update

Displays a set of symbols and other special characters

The buttons

Fe Makes lower case letters the same height as capitals.

◀ Rotates the text through 90 degrees.

▨ Makes the text expand to fill the shape.

▨ Sets the tracking – the spacing between characters.

C Sets rotation and arc angles through the Special Effects panel (see right).

▨ Sets the fill patterns for the letters.

▨ Sets the shadow style (see right).

▥ Sets the style of the outline of the letters.

This has been curved, with the arc flattened to 30°, then given a fill pattern, thin outline and simple black shadow.

Text effects

These can all be set from the toolbar – either from the buttons or the three drop-down lists. The font and size lists as are normal, except that there is a **Best Fit** size – generally the best option. The leftmost list is new.

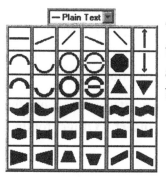

This sets the overall shape made by the text. The shape may occupy only a small part of the object's outline – be prepared to resize it.

With curved text, a smaller Arc Angle flattens the curve.

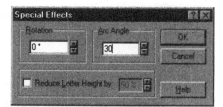

The on-the-ground shadows do not work well with shaped text. Keep these for straight text.

Spreadsheets

The formatting facilities in the spreadsheet are not bad, but if you want a really good-looking report with charts and/or tables of figures, the simplest solution is to write the report text in the word processor then insert a spreadsheet into the document.

● There is a **Spreadsheet...** option on the **Insert** menu. Use this if you are creating the spreadsheet from scratch, specially for the document, or if you want to copy in selected blocks of data from an existing sheet.

● If the spreadsheet exists, and you want to use it all, use the **Create from File** option in the **Insert – Object** routine.

1 From the Insert menu select Spreadsheet.

Or

2 Use Insert – Object... then take the Create from File option and select the file.

3 Enter/edit and format the data as required.

4 Drag on a handle to adjust the size of the spreadsheet object to suit the display.

5 Click into the document to return to word processing.

6 Double-click on the spreadsheet if you want to edit it.

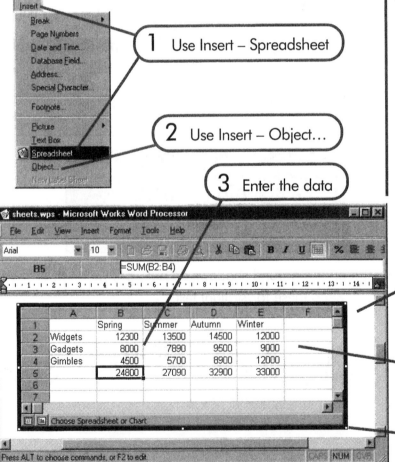

1 Use Insert – Spreadsheet

2 Use Insert – Object...

3 Enter the data

5 Return to word processing

6 Double-click to edit

4 Adjust the size

Basic steps

Charts

1 Enter the table of data and headings, if necessary, then select it.

2 Open the Tools menu and select Create New Chart..., setting options as required.

3 Format the display – note that the toolbar now has Chart tools.

4 Adjust the chart size.

5 Use the icons in the bottom left to switch between chart and spreadsheet.

The normal charting facilities are available with an embedded spreadsheet. Probably the main point to note here is that – as in the spreadsheet application – you can only display either the chart or the sheet at any one time.

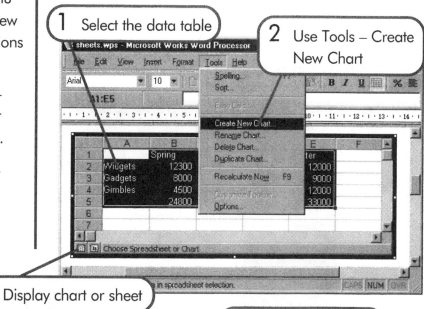

1 Select the data table

2 Use Tools – Create New Chart

5 Display chart or sheet

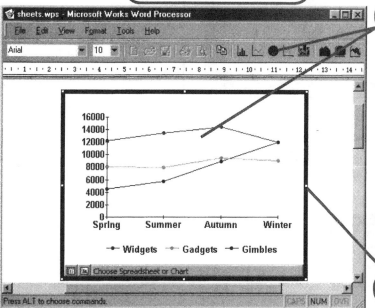

3 Format the display

4 Adjust the size

Tip

If you want to display both data and chart, insert the sheet twice, or copy it, and use one object for the figures and the other for the chart.

Mail merge

With Mail merge, you take information from a database – or from the Address Book – and slot it into a standard layout to produce mailing labels or personalised letters. With Works, a mail merge is simple to organise. The difficult part is composing a letter that people do not throw straight into the bin.

1 If you are using a database, open it and filter or mark the records that you want.

2 Start up a new document for your label or form letter.

3 Write your text, stopping when you get to where you want to pull in data. Open the Insert menu and select Database Field...

Or

4 Open the Tools menu, point to Mail Merge and select Open Data Source.

5 Select the source – either the Address Book or another type of file.

6 If using a database, select and open the file.

7 If the Insert Fields dialog box is not open, use Insert – Database Field... to open it now.

> 3 Locate the cursor and select Insert – Database Field...

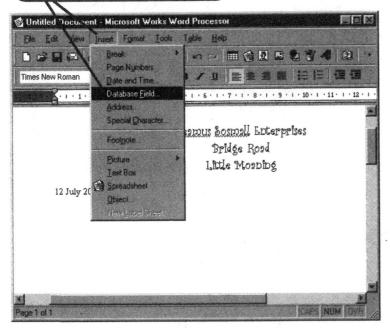

> 4 Use Tools – Mail Merge – Open Data Source.....

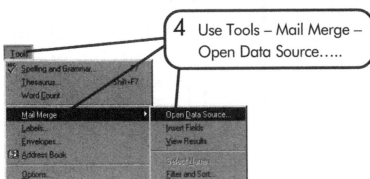

8 Select a field and click Insert.

9 Repeat step 8 to add other fields – you can edit the text, e.g. to add spaces or punctuation between the fields, without closing the Insert Fields dialog box.

10 Click ☒ when you have finished to return to the text.

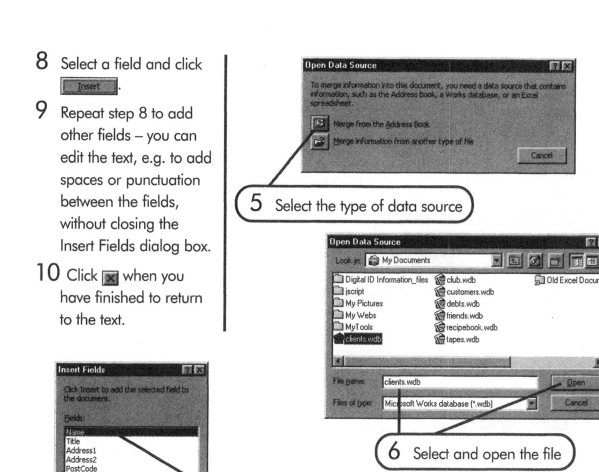

⑤ Select the type of data source

⑥ Select and open the file

⑧ Select and insert each field

⑩ Return to the text

The Insert Fields dialog box for a simple database (above) and the Address Book (right)

Take note

A database field can be moved, formatted or deleted in the same way as normal text.

Selective merging

You probably will not want to send the letter to everyone in your database or Address Book. Recipients can be picked directly from the Address Book; with a database, either mark them first or set up a filter to select them.

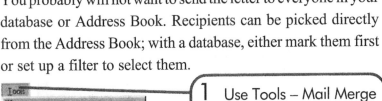

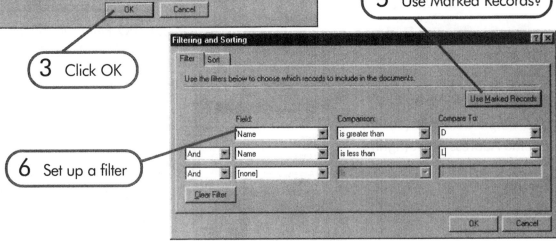

Basic steps

❑ Using the Address Book

1 Open the Tools menu, point to Mail Merge and choose Select Names...

2 Pick the recipients and click Select ->.

3 Click OK.

❑ Using a database

4 Open the Tools menu, point to Mail Merge and select Filter and Sort...

5 Click Use Marked Records.

Or

6 Set up a filter, as shown on page 110.

Basic steps

1 Open the Tools menu, point to Mail Merge and use View Results.

2 Click the arrows to move through the records.

Or

3 Use File – Print Preview and scroll through to see the different pages.

4 Print as normal.

Previewing and printing

You should always preview the letter to check that you have inserted the right fields in the right places, and that copies are going to the right people.

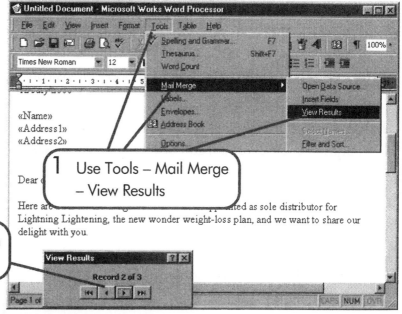

1 Use Tools – Mail Merge – View Results

2 Move through the records

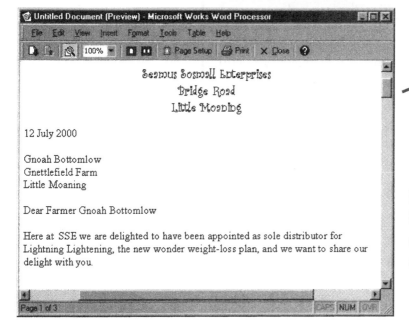

3 Scroll through the pages

Preview of the mail merge letter, showing a customer's details drawn from the database

Summary

- ❑ Objects can be inserted into word processor documents and database forms. Double-click on them or use Edit – Object to reopen the application that created them.

- ❑ Objects can be resized and repositioned. They can sit in lines free of text or have text wrapped round them.

- ❑ Objects produced by other Windows applications can be linked into your files.

- ❑ The Clip Art Gallery has hundreds of ready-made images to choose from. It can also handle any others you have on your system.

- ❑ With Draw you can build up pictures out of lines, circles, rectangles and closed polygons.

- ❑ WordArt can produce text that is curved, shaped, stretched, shadowed and patterned.

- ❑ You can insert or create new Charts or Spreadsheet within the word-processor, using the normal spreadsheet facilities.

- ❑ By inserting Database Fields into a form letter, you can create mail merge documents. The details can be taken from a database or from the Address Book.

9 Other works

Calendar

The Calendar gives you a simple but effective means to record appointments, with reminders to tell you when they are due.

The Calendar can be viewed in several ways, and the Category Filter lets you choose the type of appointments to be displayed.

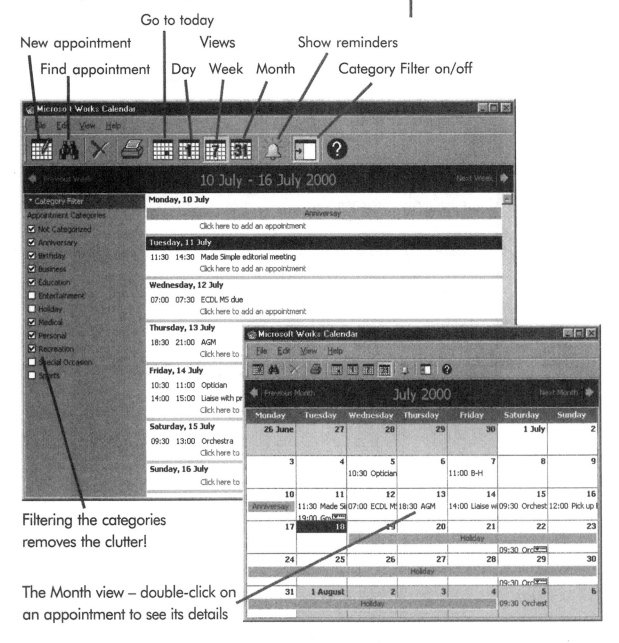

Go to today

New appointment

Views

Show reminders

Find appointment   Day Week Month   Category Filter on/off

Filtering the categories removes the clutter!

The Month view – double-click on an appointment to see its details

Basic steps

1 Double-click on the day.

2 Enter the Title – this will appear in Calendar.

3 Enter the Location if useful.

4 Click [Change...].

5 Select the category.

6 Set the start and end times from the drop-down lists.

7 To set a Reminder, pick the warning time from the drop-down list.

8 Add notes if needed.

9 Click [OK].

Tick here if it lasts all day

Making a date

A simple appointment can be set up in seconds.

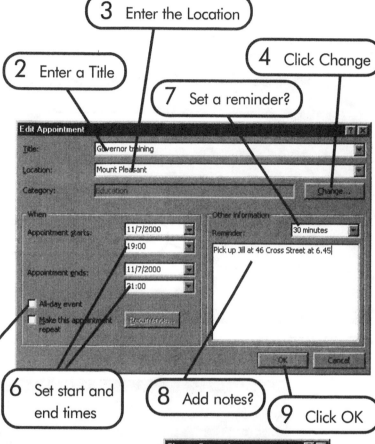

3 Enter the Location

2 Enter a Title

4 Click Change

7 Set a reminder?

6 Set start and end times

8 Add notes?

9 Click OK

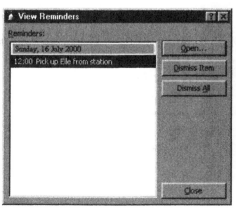

Reminders pop up on screen at the set time – as long as Calendar is running

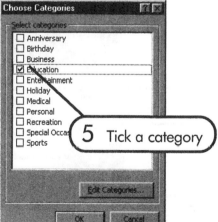

5 Tick a category

Recurring appointments

If you have a series of regular appointments, you can set them all up in one operation.

1 Set up the first date

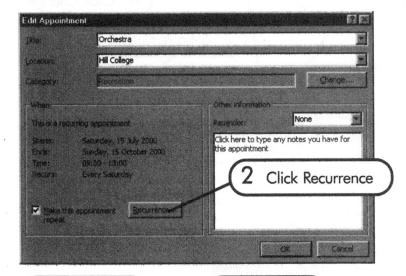

2 Click Recurrence

3 How often?

4 Set the day

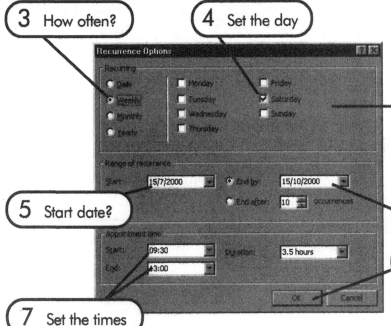

5 Start date?

6 End date?

7 Set the times

8 Click OK

Basic steps

1 Follow steps 1 to 8 on the previous page to set the day and time of the first appointment of the series.

2 Tick Make this appointment repeat then click Recurrence.

3 In Recurring set the frequency.

4 Set the Day of the week, month or year.

5 Check the Start date.

6 Set the End by date, or the End after number.

7 Check the times.

8 Click OK.

This panel is different for daily/monthly/yearly events

Basic steps

1 Start the Address Book.

2 Click New then select New Contact …

3 Enter the First, Middle and Last names – contacts are normally listed alphabetically.

4 Type the address and click ▭ Add ▭.

5 If the person has several addresses, add them and set one as the Default.

6 Click ▭ OK ▭.

Typing e-mail addresses is a pain – one slip and the mail comes bouncing back the next day with a 'recipient unknown' label. The simple solution is to use the Address Book. Type the address in once correctly – or add it when replying to a message (page 144) – and it's there whenever you want it.

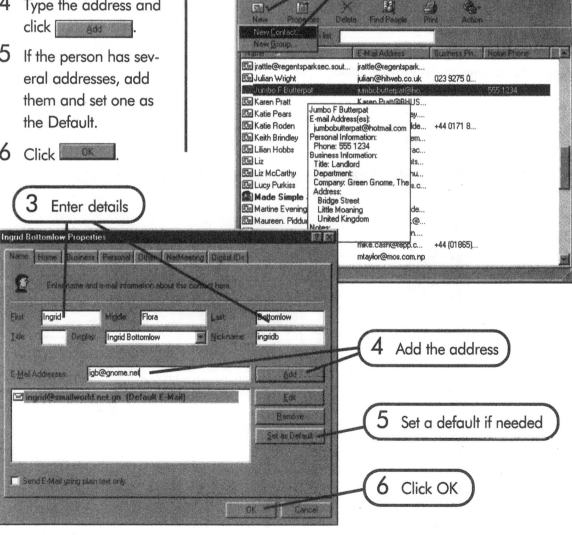

2 Use New – New Contact

3 Enter details

4 Add the address

5 Set a default if needed

6 Click OK

Outlook Express

Outlook Express is the easy to use, but very efficient mail and news application, that is supplied with Windows and Internet Explorer. To use it, you must have an e-mail account with an Internet Service Provider. There is not enough space in this book to go into the business of getting on-line – if you need help with this, please see *Internet Explorer 5 Made Simple* or *The Internet Made Simple*.

Reading mail

To read your new incoming mail, select the Inbox in the Folder list of Outlook bar, and click on a header in the Header pane to display its message in the Preview pane.

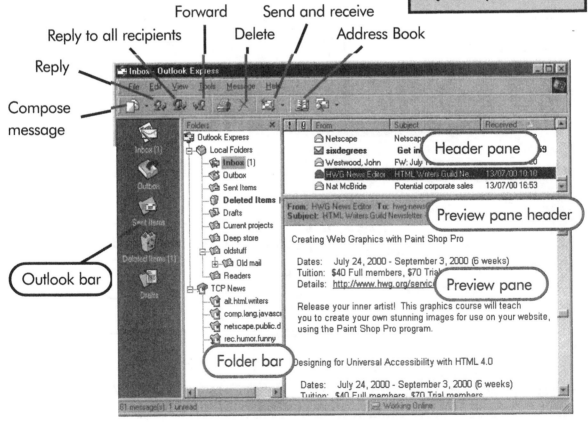

140

Basic steps

1 Open the View menu, select Layout...

2 Set the screen layout.

3 Open the View menu, and select Columns...

4 Click the checkbox to display or remove the tick, to add or remove a column from the display.

5 Select a column and use the Move Up and Down buttons to change its position.

6 Click [OK].

Display options

You can set the layout and what to include in the headers.

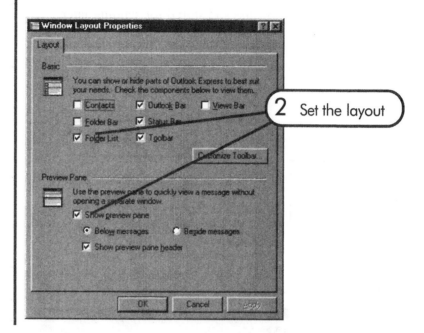

2 Set the layout

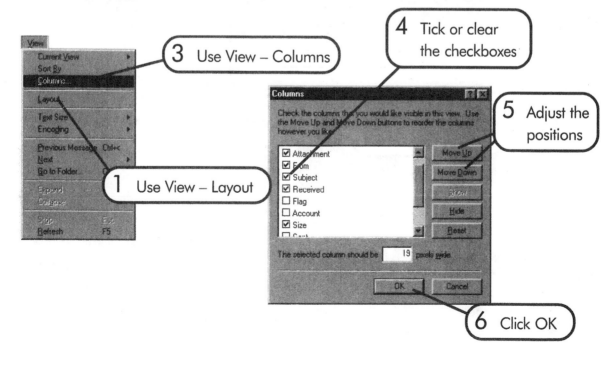

3 Use View – Columns

4 Tick or clear the checkboxes

5 Adjust the positions

1 Use View – Layout

6 Click OK

Sending messages

To send e-mail, all you need is the address – and something to say! Messages can be composed and sent immediately if you are online, or composed offline and stored for sending later.

To add impact, write your message on appropriate stationery. These have text formats and backgrounds all ready for you.

1 Select your stationery

3 Select recipients from your address book

2 Type the address

1 Click the arrow beside New Message and select a stationery style.

❏ Use No stationery – or simply click ▣ for plain paper.

2 Type the address in the To: slot.

or

3 Click ▦ beside To: to open the Select Recipients panel.

4 Select a name and click the To: button, then ▭ OK to return to the New Message window.

❏ To send copies, repeat from step 2 for the Cc: text box.

Take note

Subject lines matter as they help recipients to organise their messages. Make them brief, but clear.

5 Type a Subject.

6 Type your message.

7 Click 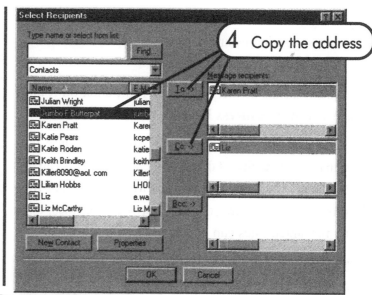.

or

8 Open the File menu and select Send Message, for immediate delivery, or Send Later.

9 Your spelling will be checked before the message is sent.

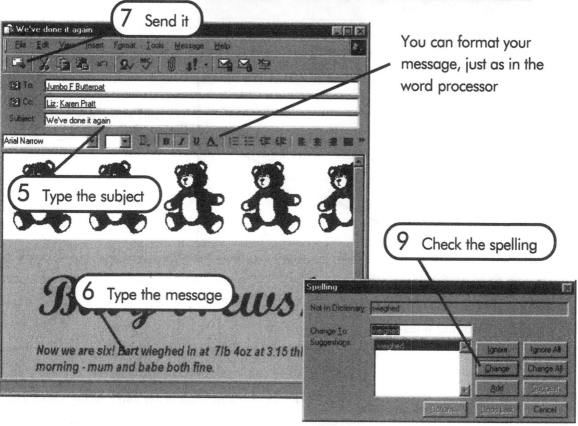

You can format your message, just as in the word processor

4 Copy the address

7 Send it

5 Type the subject

6 Type the message

9 Check the spelling

Replying

When you reply to an incoming message, the system will open the New Message window and copy the sender's address into the To: text box.

- If you want the sender's address, right-click on it and select **Add to Address Book** from the short menu.

- The original message is normally also copied into the main text area with > at the start of each line. This can be very handy if you want to respond to the mail point-by-point. You can insert your text between the lines, and any unwanted lines can be deleted.

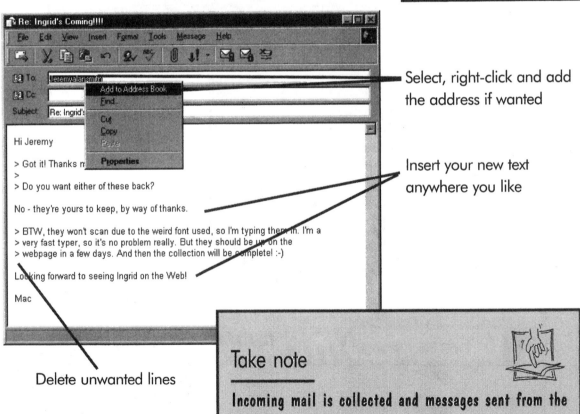

Select, right-click and add the address if wanted

Insert your new text anywhere you like

Delete unwanted lines

Forward

You can send a message on to another person – perhaps after adding your own comments to it.

❑ Forwarding mail

1 Select the message in the header pane.

2 Click ![forward] the Forward button.

3 Type or select the address(es) of the recipient(s).

4 Delete any unwanted headers or other text and add your own comments.

5 Click ![send].

Reply to all

If you get a message that has been sent to several people, you can reply to all those listed in the **To:** and **Cc:** boxes. Click ![reply all], instead of ![reply], and continue as for a normal reply. Your message will be copied to all the recipients of the original message.

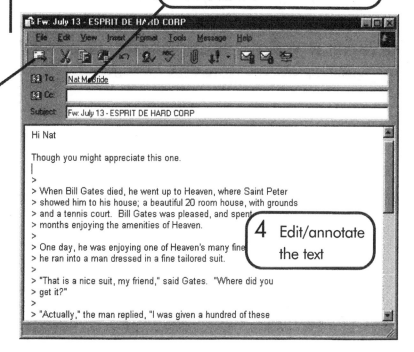

Take note

There's more to Outlook Express that can be covered here. To get further into this application, read *Internet Explorer 5 Made Simple.*

Summary

❑ Record your appointments in the Calendar and you need never miss another one!

❑ Use your Address Book and you will only ever have to type a person's e-mail address once – if at all.

❑ Use the Inbox to fetch and reply to your e-mail.

❑ Outlook Express is an e-mail application. You can customise its display to suit yourself – only the header pane is essential.

❑ When sending messages, start by selecting who they will go to. You should always write the nature of the message in the Subject line.

❑ When replying, the mail system can copy in the original message for you to add your comments to.

❑ As well as replying directly to the sender, you can reply to all recipients and forward the message on.

Index

Printed and bound by CPI Group (UK) Ltd, Croydon, CR0 4YY

17/10/2024

01775677-0009